KEFALONIA AND ITHAKI

30 April 1999

To Dr. Eug. Myers
with my best wishes,
looking forward to
see you in Greece.
N. Papadimatos

2nd EDITION

Betty Kagia

Kefalonia and Ithaki

Grecocard Publications
Athens, 1994

Editor: George Monemvassitis
General Text Supervision: Betty Kagia
Photography: A. Rodopoulos, L. Hapsis, P. Voukouris, S. Papadatos
Colour Separation: Fotokitaro Ltd.
Maps and Plans: SI Advertising
Printing and Binding: S. Nanos & Co. S.A.
ISBN 960-7436-01-6

Dear readers,

As you will discover on reading this book, I have attempted to compile under one cover written records of history and folklore in combination with data gleaned from oral tradition. I have also attempted, without sacrificing scientific accuracy on basic historical and social points, to create pleasant but informative reading matter for islanders and visitors alike. During my few days' stay on the two islands, I tried to collect as much information as possible. I finished my research in Athens, always with the help of friends from Kefalonia who have stood by me all this time. I hope that readers will view my efforts favourably. I would also like to stress that in spite of my honest endeavors and my love for the island, unintentional errors or omissions may have occurred: with your help they can be avoided in future editions.

I feel obliged to inform you that this book would never have come about without the help of the islanders, eponymous and anonymous, who by contributing invaluable information have filled these pages with their knowledge and love of the islands. In particular, I would like to thank the following Kefalonians:
Stelios Politis, Nomarch of Kefallonia and Ithaki; Evangelos Andreatos, geologist; Gerassimos Galanos, educator; Ioannis Papadatos, teacher; Stavros Papadatos, television producer; Gerassimos Moustakis, president of Agia Efimia and Moustakis; Andreas Zapantis, president of Skala; Gerassimos Metaxas, president of Poros; Ioannis Thomas, president of Fiskardo; Vassilios Loukeris, head of the Tipaldon-Iakovaton Library; Aliki Panou, of the Society for the Protection of Nature; Eleni Kosmetatou, head of the Korgialenios Museum; Vassilios Frangiskatos, shop owner; Andreas Vergotis, shipowner; Antonis Magoulas, accountant; Maria Soldatou, employee of the Korgialenios Library; my relatives in Kefalonia; the employees of the Greek National Tourist Organisation in Argostoli for the information I got from their lists of hotels, rented rooms and transport.

I would also like to thank the following people in Ithaki:
S. S. Kouvaras, teacher; Ioannis Matarangas, employee of the Greek Telecommunications Organisation; Andreas Anagnostatos, author.

Betty Kagia

Table of Contents

Introduction

With an area of 688.8 square kilometers, Kefalonia is the largest island in the Ionian Sea and sixth in size of all the Greek islands. It lies opposite the mouth of the Gulf of Patras, between Zakinthos and Lefkada. To the northeast of Kefalonia is Ithaki; the two islands are separated by a channel 3-4 km wide.

Kefalonia is made up of four peninsulas, Paliki, Erissos, Livathos and Atros. It is for the most part mountainous, in fact the most mountainous of the Ionian islands, with the highest peaks. In the southwest looms the Ainos range, whose highest peak is Megas Soros at 1.628 m. This mountain massif was in the past blanketed in vast forests of Cephalonian Fir. Most of the island's other mountains, including Mts. Roudi, Sella, Vrohonas, Avgo and Omorfia, are not much over 1,000 m in height.

Geologically, the island consists chiefly of permeable stratified rock, mainly calcareous. Subterranean caverns and passages have been formed by erosion and the dissolving action of underground water on calcareous rock (Karst topography). The peculiarity of this rock permits water to be diffused through it at attainable levels, so that even the inhabitants of mountainous areas can find water easily. In fact, the island is believed to have once had such an abundance of water that its mountains were clothed in thick forests of a dark green colour – hence one of its ancient names, Melaina, from melanos=black. The streams and torrents that flow down from the mountains empty into the sea, except for those in the area of Omala and Pirgi. They form Lake Avithos (Megali Akoli) and Mikri Akoli; the latter has all but dried up and collects some water only in times of heavy rains.

Crenellated shores and well-proportioned peninsulas grace the island's coasts

Kefalonia's plains are small and few in number; two examples are Livathos and Omala. In Livathos, the island's most fertile plain, chain-links and ships' accoutrements were discovered, testimony that this, like the island's other plains, once formed part of the sea-bed.

The island's countless bays and inlets have given it its odd shape and have abetted it in its maritime endeavours from the most ancient of times. Two peninsulas extend out from the centre of the island, the Erissos peninsula in the north and the Paliki peninsula to the west and south. The rocky coast of Kefalonia is interrupted frequently by spotlessly clean beaches of pebbles and sand, of which the islanders are justifiably proud.

The climate of Kefalonia is temperate and it is sunny for most of the year. Winters are mild and rainy and low temperatures range between –11 and 2 degrees C. Summers are cool and dry with minimal rainfall; the thermometer seldom reaches 40 degrees C.

The island's economy is based mainly on its agricultural produce, but also on stock-breeding. Fishing is another source of wealth, as is the tourist industry, which has been growing slowly but steadily during recent years. Some well-known products of Kefalonia are its famous Rombola wines, several varieties of grapes, cheese products, fine honey, olive oil and figs.

Together with Ithaki, Kefalonia forms the Nome of Kefalinia with a population of 32,000. Its capital is Argostoli which is also the largest town and capital of the Eparchy of Kranea. The island's second Eparchy is Paliki whose capital is Lixouri, and its third is Sami whose capital is the town of Sami. Before the great earthquake of 1953, Kefalonia alone had about 365 villages; today only 200 of them remain, most near the coast and in the few plains. The dense network of roads covering the whole island will help you get acquainted with these villages.

Kefalonia is connected to the rest of Greece via the airport in Argostoli and the harbours of Sami, Poros and Agia Efimia. It also has links with the other Ionian islands and Astakos in Epirus (see table at the end of this book).

Many islanders, living up to their title of seafarers, still fish for a living; the Ionian Sea is a good place to do it

Mythology

Many different myths are associated with the mighty kingdom of Kefalonia, or Cephalonia or Cephallenia, myths without any logical unity or chronological equilibrium. According to Apollodorus of Athens, the island's first king was Taphius, son of Poseidon and Hippothoe, daughter of Mnestor, king of the Myceneans. The first settlers of the town of Taphus were the Taphians or the Teleboans, of Pelasgian origin (Acarnanian pro-Hellenes, who first settled on the island in the 3rd millennium BC). Taphius' son was Pterelaus, whose grandfather Poseidon gave him a golden hair which made him immortal as long as it stayed on his head. When the city of Kefalonia, which had by that time become quite powerful, demanded a substantial part of the kingdom held up to then by the Myceneans (the descendants of the legendary king Perseus), their king Electryon refused. In retaliation, the Taphians stole his flocks. Electryon never forgave them, and when Amphitryon, king of Thebes, asked for his daughter Alcmene's hand in marriage, Electryon agreed, on the condition that Amphitryon take revenge for him. Amphitryon, aided by Cephalus and Eleius, set out to conquer Taphus. They never would have defeated the immortal king, had it not been for Comaetho, the daughter of Pterelaus, who fell in love with Amphitryon. One night as her father lay sleeping she cut the magic hair off his head. Pterelaus, now mortal, was defeated, his treacherous daughter put to death, and Amphitryon returned to Thebes after handing over the spoils to his fellow-warrior, Cephalus.

Just who was that mythical hero Cephalus, who gave the island his name? Apollodorus informs us that Cephalus was the son of Hermes and Herse, the daughter of Cecrops, and that he belonged to the race of Cephalidae from Thoricus in Attica. (There are, however, suspicions that the myth was invented for political purposes by the Athenians in the 5th century BC.) Another myth has it that Cephalus was the son of the king of Phokis, Deioneus, and yet another presents him as the son of Pandion and Creusa.

Numerous myths have been invented about the erotic and marital adventures of Cephalus, a handsome man and intrepid hunter. He married Procris, daughter of the king of Attica Erechtheus and Praxithea. Cephalus was very much in love with her. Ovid tells the following story: It was during the second month of their marriage, and Cephalus "was spreading his nets on the peak of Mt. Hymettus to catch deer with big antlers", when Eos (the Dawn) appeared before

Mythical Cephalus and his hunting-dog Laelaps on a lekythos dating from 480 BC (London, British Museum)

him in a chariot with the intention of kidnapping him. In vain did the poor mortal struggle against the goddess, pleading his recent marriage and his love for his legal wife. Finally the goddess, seeing him so unwilling, freed him, but not until she had sown a few doubts about his wife's fidelity. In disguise, the suspicious husband returned to his wife and offered her his treasures. When her categorical refusal slowly began to falter, Cephalus, furious, revealed his true identity. The shamed wife went off to live in the mountains of Crete, where she became a huntress. Artemis, seeing that she was repentant, gave her a hunting dog, Laelaps, who always caught his quarry, and a spear that always found its mark. Then she turned Procris into a man and sent her home to her husband. She invited Cephalus to take part in a hunting contest and when she was victorious she revealed her true identity. The "deceived" husband realised his mistake and they lived happily together for many years.

Once the Thebans asked for Cephalus' help, because a wild beast, destined by the gods never to be vanquished by the hand of man, was wreaking havoc in the area. Cephalus took Laelaps with him and set him to hunt the beast. But as the two animals were creations of the gods, neither one could ever defeat the other. So the gods turned them to stone to save them from disgracing themselves.

Procris, however, always had a seed of jealousy in her heart, and every time her husband went hunting alone, she thought he was going out to meet Eos. So she followed him everywhere, staying hidden behind the bushes. On one of his hunting trips he mistook her for a deer and killed her with her own spear. The Areopagus sentenced the wife-killer to perpetual exile, and that was how he found himself in the friendly city of Thebes, involved in Amphitryon's expeditions against the Taphians. Some say that, inconsolable for what he had done, he threw himself over the cliff on Cape Leukata.

Another variation of the same myth tells how the wife, in her shame, took refuge in Crete, where she proceeded to deceive her husband with Pteleon. King Minos had a spell cast on him by his wife Pasiphae: every time he embraced another woman, snakes and scorpions crawled out of his body. Procris cured him, and out of gratitude, the king presented her with Laelaps and the spear. It was Pasiphae's anger that forced Procris to return to Athens and straighten things out with Cephalus.

Apollodorus puts a little more spice in the myth. He has king Minos fall head over heels in love with Procris. In order to win her, he does not hesitate to give her the hunting dog and the spear. After that the myth continues in the usual way.

Aristotle tells us that the hero could not have children, so he asked for advice from the priestess at Delphi. The oracle recommended that he have intercourse with the first female creature he saw. That creature turned out to be a bear! That was how Arceisius, future king of the Ionian islands and part of the Acarnanian peninsula, was born. His son, Laertes, was heir to that kingdom, as was Laertes' son Odysseus after him.

The face of mythical Cephalus appears on many ancient coins. His life was a source of inspiration not only for ancient historians, but also for modern artists. (Guerin painted his abduction by Eos.) His descendents all lived up to his reputation. They were kings for ten generations, after which they returned to Attica on orders from the Delphic oracle.

Myth tells us that in Homer's time Same was first inhabited by Angaeus, who, according to Iamblichus, was descended from Zeus. The fact that Angaeus was an Arcadian hero is one more proof that the Cephallenes were of Arcadian origin. Aristotle tells us that he was a "friend of agriculture" and was the first to cultivate the vine. It is also said that because he was of an advanced age, one of his servants admonished him not to get too tired, so that he would live to drink the wine from his grapes. When the time of the grape harvest arrived, the king called his servant to show him that he would drink some of his wine. The wise servant's reply was proverbial: "Many things can happen before you put the cup to your lips." And indeed, at that moment another servant arrived to tell the king that a wild boar had appeared in the town and was causing damage and injuring people. When the king hurried off to kill it, he was wounded and died.

The inhabitants of Kefalonia honoured many of the Olympian gods, which shows that they were in contact with mainland Greece. Depicted on coins found in all four city-states of Kefalonia are Aenesian Zeus (who is none other than Olympian Zeus), Poseidon, from whom the Taphians were descended, Athena, protectress of Odysseus, and Demeter, goddess of agriculture. Other coins featured Cephalus, Procris, Heracles and Laelaps, who were worshipped as demi-gods.

What's in a Name

Kefalonia is believed to have taken its name from the hero Cephalus. Perhaps the name of the inhabitants, Cephaloi, comes from the word "cephales" which may refer to Kefalonia's mountains, or to the fact that it is the biggest of the Ionian islands. The Cephallenes, subjects of the legendary king Cephalus, inhabitants of a kingdom which included Kefalonia (Same), neighbouring Ithaki, Zakinthos, Lefkada and a part of Akarnania, are first mentioned by Homer. Going farther back in time, no one can say for sure whether Taphus (possibly Cephalus' town) was the name of one town or of the whole island. Up to some point, the island would appear to have been governed as a unified whole. But Homer informs us that Odysseus took part in the Trojan War with 12 ships from Samos; from this we can safely assume that other towns were created later.

Thucydides refers to these towns as the Tetrapolis. Their names – Pale, Crane, Same and Pronnoi – have come down to us in the writings of the ancient authors Thucydides and Strabo, as well as on coins and inscriptions. They were named after the four sons of Cephalus, Samos, Pronnesos, Peleus and Cranius. The ancient geographer Strabo also called Kefalonia Melaina or Melane Epirus, because of its thick, dark forests.

The name Same, taken from a Phoenician word that according to Strabo means high places, is mentioned in the Iliad in reference to the whole island.

The kingdom of Odysseus (engraving by Tardieu)

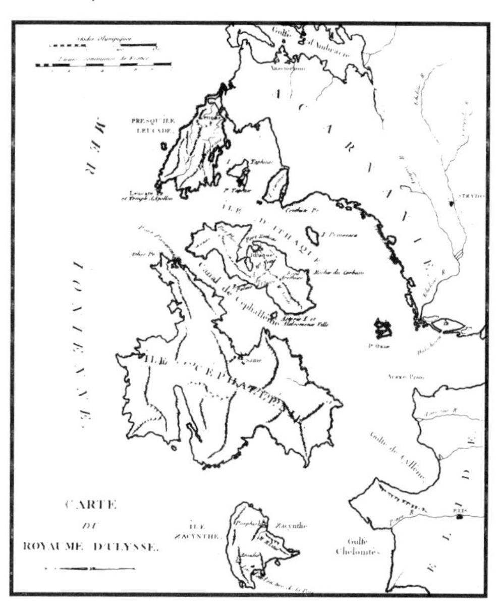

The island's thriving economy in ancient times was in large part due to the Mt. Ainos fir forest

The Island's History

Kefalonia was one of the first places in Greece to be inhabited, as shown by fossil plants, animals, bones, etc. found in Fiskardo and tools dating back to 50,000 BC discovered in Skala and Same. According to the famous Kefalonian archaeologist and professor Spiros N. Marinatos (1901-1974), all the conditions were present in Kefalonia to make it inhabitable. At a time when trade was in its infancy, one of these conditions was that the motherland itself produce everything necessary for survival. Kefalonia was the breadbasket of the other Ionian islands. It also produced olive oil, wine and fruit. Its vast forests provided plenty of timber to build ships and develop trade. During Mycenean times and the age of Homer, the island undoubtedly derived a good part of its wealth from the forest of Ainos. Recent research has proved that the columns in the palace at Knossos were made of Cephalonian Fir! This in turn proves the existence of trade. Moreover, Kefalonia's geographical position made it a stepping-stone between East and West. The Kefalonian archaeologist and academician P. Kavadias stresses the similarity between the inhabitants of the colony of Fiskardo with peoples from neighbouring Epirus, the Peloponnese and southern Italy (Pelasgian tribes). From the pre-Mycenean and Mycenean tombs in Lakithra we may draw the conclusion that they were a bellicose people; anthropological examination of skulls has revealed that most of them had suffered repeated blows.

It is quite apparent that the whole island was inhabited by the middle of the 11th century BC (organised burial grounds). That was the about the time that Cephalus and the name Cephalonia appeared. Around 1300 BC, Achaeans from Arcadia and Trifyllia in the western Peloponnese began to found colonies farther afield, in Crete, Cyprus and even Sicily. The Achaeans were a people who formerly had lived in Minyan Orchomenus in Thessaly which according to Homer was the most important city in Mycenean Greece. Some of them wound up in Kefalonia, bringing Mycenean civilisation, gods and heroes along with them. Finds from their settlements, the most thriving

Prehistoric finds from various parts of Kefalonia (Argostoli Archaeological Museum)

of which were in Crane, testify to links with the Peloponnese. From the middle of the 11th century up to the middle of the 8th century BC nothing has been found. After that the evidence points to continuous human presence on the island.

Historical Era

It would appear that in Kefalonia, as in the rest of Greece, when monarchy went into decline, oligarchies came into being. Around the 8th century BC the oligarchies had evolved into tyrannies and by the end of the 7th century BC they had become democracies.

After the decline of tyranny, Kefalonia split into four city-states, which Thucydides tells us were autonomous. Their relations with each other were not always friendly, as the existence of city walls and different coinage would indicate.

The first city-state to appear on the political scene was Pale. In his Histories, Herodotus tell us that in 479 BC the Paleans sent 200 hoplites to fight the Persians in the battle at Plataea. Pale was the first port of call for the Corinthians on their way to Sicily; thus the two cities had a strong bond of friendship. In 435 BC the Paleans again appeared on the scene, sending 4 ships to help the Corinthians fight the Corcyraeans.

During the Peloponnesian War (431-404 BC) all four cities were free allies of the Athenians. The Athenians, however, do not seem to have trusted them completely, because before a year had passed 150 Athenian triremes sailed out to attack the Peloponnese and Acarnania. In the end they took Kefalonia without resistance and made the island their base of operations against Corinth. The following year, 40 Corinthian triremes and 1500 hoplites landed in Crane. The Cranians pretended to be ready to negotiate and then in a surprise attack routed the invaders. Later, we will see on countless occasions how the Kefalonians used diplomacy in a similar way to deal with such threats and thus ensure their independence. This was just the beginning of a long train of conquerors of many races, who left their mark on the island's bloodstained history, but never managed to change its identity.

At the end of the first Peloponnesian War in 404 BC the Ionian islands found themselves on the side of Sparta. But when Athens had shaken off her tyrants, her fleet took Kefalonia and imposed heavy taxation. In 378 BC Athens set up the Second Athenian Confederacy, more liberal than the first. This situation did not last long, however, because in the following year the Athenians sank the Spartan fleet and subjugated the Ionian islands without bloodshed.

In 337 BC, when Philip conquered Greece and sent out invitations to the assembly of the Greeks in Corinth, Kefalonia sent representatives. The island remained loyal to the Macedonians during the battle of Lamia between the Greeks and the Macedonians in 323-322 BC, and remained independent throughout this period.

After the death of Alexander the Great, Kefalonia entered into an alliance with the Aetolian League. This alliance was advantageous both to the Aetolians, as they were ensured of a safe port from which to sail towards Italy and Sicily, and to the Kefalonians, because it offered them an opportunity to engage in profitable piratical activities. The Aetolians, with the help of their allies including Kefalonia and Zakinthos, caused great havoc in the rich lands of the Achaeans and their allies. The Achaeans finally enlisted the help of Philip V of Macedonia. During the War of the Allies (220-217 BC), the Macedonian king, mindful of Kefalonia's strategic position, decided to concentrate on it first; his fleet put in at Pronnoi in 218 BC. But because that part

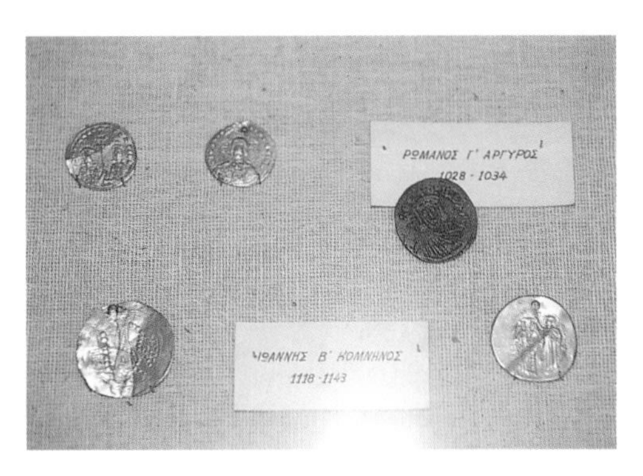

Gold and bronze Byzantine coins (Argostoli Archaeological Museum)

of the island was deemed hard to conquer, he turned to Pale, the most powerful city, in the most fertile area of the island. The Macedonians failed, however, to conquer it, despite Philip's many stratagems. On the other side, when the Aetolians and their allies learned about the attempt to beseige Pale, they immediately began launching attacks on Achaean territory in an attempt to draw the attention of their opponents away from Kefalonia.

Roman and Byzantine Times

After the Second Punic War (202 BC), the Romans were casting about for a way to revenge themselves on Philip for entering into an alliance with the Carthaginian general Hannibal. Pretexts were quickly found, but the underlying reason was Rome's designs for expansion in Greece. War broke out in 200 BC; initially, the Aetolians and their allies remained neutral. But because their neutrality turned out to be advantageous to Philip, they allied themselves with the Romans against him. Disappointed in a relationship which had promised a lot but proved to be of little profit to them, they entered into an alliance with the Greek king in Syria Antiochus III. That gave Rome to go-ahead to conquer Odysseus' celebrated land, motivated more by ambition than anything else. Thus in 198 BC the Romans sent the consul M. Fulvius Nobili to Kefalonia to ask its four cities to surrender and hand over 20 prominent citizens as hostages. When the hostages had been delivered and everything appeared calm, the city of Same closed its gates. Titus Livius writes that the Samians' reaction was spurred by a rumor that the Romans intended to evacuate the city and move in themselves. The seige lasted four months. Finally the exhausted Samians were forced to surrender in 189 BC. Between then and 30 BC, Kefalonia lost everything it had gained from its alliance with the Aetolians. Just as they had planned, the Romans turned the island into a base of operations from which their naval forces could patrol the area of Greece.

When Constantine reorganised the Roman Empire in 325 AD, Kefalonia became part of the Eparchy of Achaea. Attacks by barbarians (Vandals and Ostrogoths), as well as mandatory involvement in the Romans' wars with African emperors, often put the island in danger. The next time the empire was reorganised, under the emperor Heraclius in 629-634, it was divided into smaller themes (districts) which afforded it better protection from its enemies. Kefalonia then became the seat of the islands belonging to the Theme of Lombardy, the most important in Europe, and thus regained some of her old prestige and wealth. This Theme, with its powerful navy, was often instrumental in repelling Arab attacks on the Empire.

Under the Emperor Nicephorus I (802-811), the Theme of Lombardy was eliminated and the Theme of Calabria set up; it became the target of repeated attacks by Saracen and Andalusian pirates. In 887 the Emperor Leon the Wise established the Theme of Cephallenia, whose capital was at Pale. The island regained its prominent position, and kept it for another 300 years. It was again fortified, and served as a defense bastion of the empire. When Nicephorus Phocas defeated the Arabs in Crete in 961, the Ionian islands were relieved of pirate raids and they prospered until the Normans appeared on the scene.

The Norman Occupation

The Normans (of German origin) lived in the Scandinavian peninsula. In 1057 Robert Guiscard became their sovereign. When Nicephorus Botaniatus deposed the Emperor Michael VII and locked up his wife Eleni, Guiscard's daughter, in a monastery, the Normans had all the pretext they needed. They assembled an army and fleet in 1081, and attacked the Ionian islands. The Byzantine fleet was defeated and Corcyra taken by an artifice. To Robert's son fell the difficult task of conquering Kefalonia (Pale). But when Robert heard that his son's efforts had proved unsuccessful, he set sail for Kefalonia. The strain was too much for his heart, however, and on July 17, 1085 he died near Cape Panormos in Kefalonia. The resistance of the islanders rendered the grandiose plans of ambitious Robert fruitless and marked the end of Norman attacks.

Robert's other son, Bohemund, sought aid from powerful seafaring cities in Italy. Thus, late in 1103 the Ionian islands were attacked by the Pisans. When the Emperor Ioannes ratified certain naval privileges he had granted to the Venetians, Corcyra and Kefalonia were attacked, in 1122 and 1124 respectively. His successor, Manuel I, who believed the fleet to be less important than the army, was unable to offer the islands any help. Left without help and suffering from a lack of food, the islands were forced to surrender a year later. Manuel's successor, I. Kaloioannes, immediately took Kefalonia again, returning to the Venetians everything that had been taken from them.

When Manuel Andronicus I took the throne by slaughtering the lawful heir along with many Italian citizens, the king of Lower Italy and Sicily, William II, entered into an alliance with the Normans against Byzantium. The suspicious emperor had incompetent generals and garrison commanders, who could only offer minimal help at the moment of crisis.

In July 1185, the admiral of the Norman fleet and former corsair, Margaritonis, took Corcyra and Kefalonia without a fight and dissolved the Theme of Cephallenia. Hundreds of people were massacred, hostages were taken and property seized. Margaritonis was made a count for his services. The new capital of the islands was again in Kefalonia, but this time it was in the fortress of Agios Georgios, and not the fortress of Pale.

The heirs to the kingdoms of Sicily and Normandy did not keep up the friendly relations of their predecessors. In the battle between them, Margaritonis took the side of the Normans, and after their defeat he went off to become a pirate again. Pursued by the German Emperor Heinrich VI, he was captured and blinded, and died in Germany in 1194. His successor, Matteo Orsini, a pirate himself, abolished the Orthodox diocese and chose a Latin bishop in order to be on better terms with the Pope.

The Frankish Conquest

In 1204 the Crusaders and the Venetians signed an agreement in Constantinople dividing up the Byzantine Empire. The islands passed into Venetian hands. In 1236 Matteo Orsini declared allegiance to the principality of Achaea. In 1258 his son, Ricardo, succeeded him; he was no less cunning than his father.

He used his wiles to marry his son, Ioannes I, to the daughter of the Despot of Epirus, who became Count of Kefalonia upon his father's death in 1303. Ioannes' first-born son, Nicolaus, was not only heir to his father's holdings, but he murdered the despot of Epirus and took his title. In 1323 his brother, Ioannes II, murdered him for his titles, but he didn't stop there. He usurped his sister's dowry and the property of her husband, William Tocco, which amounted to half of the island of Zakinthos. He acknowledged the Emperor Andronicus II as his sovereign and to increase his popularity renounced the Orsini lineage and adopted the name Ioannes Angelus Commenus. Upon learning of these events, the d'Anjou kings of Naples demanded that Ioannes take an oath of allegiance. When he refused, the king of Naples married the widow of the prince of Achaea to the Count of Gravina and sent him to fight Ioannes Commenus. In 1335 Ioannes' wife poisoned him. His son Nicephorus reigned for only two years (1356-1358).

In 1357 the king of Naples gave Leonardo I Tocco the islands of Kefalonia, Zakinthos, Ithaki, Lefkada and Vonitsa as a reward for his services. His successor, Carolus I, added them to his holdings in Epirus. Carolus I died in 1429 and was succeeded by his nephew, Carolus II. In order to save what he could from the Turks, Carolus II ceded the town of Ioannina to them. They were not appeased, however; in 1442 they seized control of Zakinthos and the Peloponnese. In 1448 Carolus II died and his son Leonard III, still a child, took the throne. Leonard sought help from the Venetians in regaining his lost territories. He reinstituted the Orthodox diocese which had been abolished and refused to pay the onerous taxes imposed by the treaty between the Venetians and the Turks. Pursued by the Turks, Leonard retreated

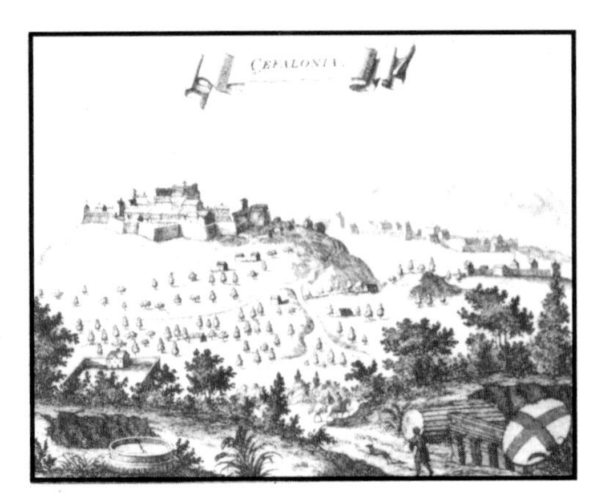

The castle of Agios Georgios, from the Anville collection

to Neapoli. The Ionian islands, with the exception of Corcyra, fell into Turkish hands in 1479.

The brother of Leonard III, Antonius, took Kefalonia back in 1481, but he was so tyrannical that the Kefalonians killed him and surrendered to the Venetians. In the treaty of April 22, 1485, Kefalonia was ceded to the Turks. This period was one of the worst the island has ever known.

Venetian Rule

During the second war between Turkey and Venice (1499-1502) the fortress of Agios Georgios was beseiged and rebuilt. In 1504, a new treaty gave Venice control of the island. Thus, while the rest of Greece was bowing beneath the Turkish yoke, the Ionian islands were governed by the more civilised Venetians. They granted tax exemptions and land to brave warriors and settlers from Turkish-controlled areas. They also encouraged cultivation of grapes for raisins, which brought ships from many countries to Kefalonia. (From Venetian times up to the early 1900s Kefalonia produced 10,000 tons of raisins annually.)

In 1537 Suleiman the Magnificent declared war on Venice. This was when

The entrance to the Assos fortress with Venetian emblems at the top

the notorious Khayr al-Din Barbarossa, pirate and later admiral of the Turkish fleet, first made his appearance. In the wake of his attack on the Ionian islands and Parga, the allies found nothing but corpses and rubble.

In 1540 Venice concluded a humiliating peace with Suleiman. But there was no peace for Kefalonia, because Dragoutos, one of Barbarossa's chieftains, attacked the island repeatedly. Another large-scale assault by admiral Ali Pasha in 1571 was directed at Same, Erissos and Thinea, wreaking fearsome destruction; the fortress of Agios Georgios was not attacked as it was considered impregnable.

Two years later the Venetians and the Turks concluded a peace. Throughout these times pirate raids continued – some of them instigated by other European states out of hatred for Venice and her possessions. To deal with such threats, the fortress of Assos was erected in 1593. After the battle of Naupactus in 1571, Algerian pirate raids subsided and trade and shipping began to increase. At that time, Kefalonia had over 200 large and 5,000 small ships plying the seas. But because the authorities were installed in the fortress, sanitary regulations were often violated and a black market came into being, which had a negative effect on the island's economy. That was why in 1603 warehouses were built in the harbour of Argostoli for use by merchants. In 1632 the area began to be settled systematically.

The 17th century saw the first of a series of disastrous earthquakes, more terrible than those the island had previously known. The 1636 quake caused great material damage and took 540 lives. In 1640 a civil war broke out among the nobility, the farmers and poor peasants, and did not cease until two years later, when Venice sent an envoy to arrest the leaders of the rebels. Two years later a similar situation developed and continued until 1645, when war broke out between Turkey and Venice over Crete. Kefalonia took part, sending troops and matériel.

The revolts continued from 1647 to 1654, but now it was not only peasants fighting against nobles, but nobles against members of the Frankish nobility who had married Greek women.

In 1658, as the islands' governor was getting ready to launch a campaign against Lefkada, which the Turks had turned into a base of operations for launching assaults on the other Ionian islands, a great earthquake shook the island and razed Lixouri, claiming 320 victims.

Despite the natural disasters that racked Kefalonia and Zakinthos, their economy flourished due to trade; Crete, now embroiled in a war with Turkey, was no longer a competitor. Censuses from that era kept in the archives of Venice show that Kefalonia's population of 70,000 was larger than that of the other Ionian islands; apart from the native Kefalonians, refugees from the Peloponnese, central Greece and even Venice had taken up residence on the island. And after the fall of Crete, Cretan families were relocated en masse on Kefalonia.

Xeropotamos or Potami torrent, which used to drain the plains behind Lixouri, a work by de Bosset (Korgialenio Museum, Argostoli)

The subjugation of Crete to the Turks enraged the Venetians, who were waiting for a pretext to attack. In 1682, Austria declared war on Turkey; two years later Venice was fighting at her side. Aided by the Kefalonians, Morosini took the fortress of Lefkada in August 1682. During the years that followed the Kefalonians often helped free other areas of Greece from the Turkish yoke.

Venice, a great power until the 16th century, went into decline in 1715 when she lost the Peloponnese. The lands in her possession were now plagued by usury, tax evasion and crime. This nasty situation came to a head in 1753, when the island's dignitaries sent Ioannis Delaportas to Venice to ask that Argostoli be made administrative centre, and it became the island's capital in 1757.

The dawn of the 18th century found Kefalonia occupied in shipbuilding and trade. In 1753 a free trade agreement was signed by the Venetian government and the pirate states (Algeria and Albania), in an attempt to combat piracy; however, this effort also proved to be fruitless.

The Russians in the Ionian Islands – French Occupation

In Kefalonia, as elsewhere, Venice had lost all her authority and prestige. In the civil war between the Anninos and Metaxas families which broke out in 1755 and lasted until 1760, the Venetian authorities did not dare intervene. It was only natural that the Kefalonians seek some other power to protect them. All eyes were turned towards Russia, insignificant before the 18th century, who had now taken her place among the important states of Europe, after Peter the Great's reforms and her attacks on the Turks. Hopes sprang up in the hearts of the Greeks that they would soon be liberated from the Turkish yoke and that Orthodoxy would be reinstated. Many Greeks decided to renounce their fatherland during that period. Those who reached the Imperial court of Russia were rewarded with glory and honours. Many Kefalonians held high office under Catherine the Great.

In 1767 an earthquake claimed 253 victims on the island.

Greek revolutionaries in Russia began to instigate rebellion in the fatherland. The Kefalonian sergeant G. Papazoglou arrived in Trieste and sent some of his men to rouse Greeks to the cause. Around the same time the Orlof brothers were meeting in Venice with Slavs and Greeks. Before long the results of their endeavours were apparent.

Russia declared war on Turkey in 1768. The Venetian authorities tried in vain to stop the uprisings and turmoil that were occurring on the islands (1770-1773). Russian victories led to the treaty of 22 July 1777, under which the rebels were granted amnesty and allowed to practice the Orthodox religion openly and Greeks in Turkey were allowed to leave the country unimpeded.

In 1789 the French revolution broke out, and its repercussions were felt in Kefalonia. In 1795 the commander of the French army Napoleon Bonaparte appeared in the arena of war; he declared war on Venice on May 1, 1797. When he had defeated her, he sent envoys to the islands to assume their military and civil administration. A democratic government known as the Demarcheion was set up in Argostoli; Demarcheia were also established in Lixouri and other farming districts. Kefalonia, Ithaki, Lefkada, Vonitsa and Preveza now constituted the Nome of Ithaki. A primary concern of the French was the improvement of the Kefalonians' intellectual life, which they brought about by founding schools, French colleges and libraries. But it would seem that the wretched state of the economy caused enthusiasm fo the status quo to wane after Bonaparte's campaign in Egypt, the Russians allied themselves with the Turks against him. The islanders could not hide their enthusiasm.

The remaining Gallophiles attacked this new faction of dissenters, and this gave the middle class a chance to rebel against the nobility; the peasants in turn refused to recognise the judiciary authorities and declared themselves free of any obligation towards the landowners.

Of course, the French continued to govern the island, and when the inhabitants of Lixouri took up arms against the central government in Argostoli, their leaders were captured and the rebellion was quelled.

In September 1798, the French guard abandoned Argostoli. On the 29th of October, the Russo-Turkish fleet landed in Argostoli and declared the Ionian islands free. In the agreement drawn up later between the Russians and Turks, the Ionian islands are mentioned as belonging to the Sublime Porte under the name of "United Septinsular State". Only nobles and well-to-do bourgeois participated in the government. Internal strife was not long in appearing. It was decided to move the judicial and sanitary authorities to Lixouri; as soon as the fleet sailed

View of Argostoli from the journal "Esperos" (G. Galanos collection)

out of the harbour, the people of Argostoli rebelled. On August 12, 1800, Omala, Livathos and Skala united against Argostoli. Lixouri was attacked the same day by the villages of Anogi. Russia was forced to send commissaries (Dessilas and Kapodistrias) to enforce the constitution, but even they were unable to restore order. Revolts, bloody conflict, firing of ships and other serious crimes not only continued but spread to the other islands. Things calmed down three years later, when the Doge Ioannis Mocenigo drew up a new constitution and imposed order, allowing trade to resume.

In 1806, when Austria, Prussia, England and Russia declared war on France, Turkey allied herself to Napoleon out of fear. The Septinsular State could not remain neutral for long. In the end the islands entered the conflict, and when the French defeated the allies at Austerlitz, a treaty was signed ceding the Ionian islands to France.

By the 8th of July, the French flag was flying over all the islands. Napoleon sent General Donzelot to Kefalonia to ensure that his possessions prospered.

A painting by the island's Swiss governor de Bosset; one of his other works is the Argostoli bridge (Korgialenio Museum)

The English in the Ionian Islands

The appearance of English cruisers in the Ionian Sea put a stop to trade and communications among the islands. The islanders' appalling living conditions made them wonder if perhaps the presence of a new power might help them throw off the foreign yoke, so they looked for a way to enable the English to take over the island. The English themselves were enthusiastic and in 1809 General John Oswald attacked and occupied Kefalonia without a fight. When the English had occupied the islands and began to protect trade, they once again began to prosper. The Swiss Colonel Charles Philippe de Bosset served as governor of Kefalonia from 1810 to 1814. During those years administration was improved and many public works carried out.

In the meantime, at the conference of Vienna the fate of Europe, along with that of the Ionian Islands, was being decided. There were many who desired to possess the islands, among them the Knights of St. John, the Pope and the English; the agent of the Tsar of Russia, Kapodistrias, proposed that they be handed over to Austria as an independent state. The treaty signed on November 6, 1815 made the islands a British protectorate under the name "United States of the Ionian Islands".

First to be appointed commissioner for the islands was Thomas Maitland. He concentrated all the legislative and executive powers in his own hands. His stern decrees did not keep the Kefalonians from forming revolutionary bodies and constituting a heroic presence in the struggle for Greek independence. Kefalonia's ships provided supplies for the fighters, the island provided a place of refuge for women and children, and volunteers formed military detachments which performed admirably in action. In addition, many of the more active members of the Friendly Society were Kefalonians. Another Kefalonian was Captain Marinos Sklavos, who removed the body of the Patriarch Gregorius V from the Bosporus; the Turks had hanged him and thrown his body into the sea.

Kefalonia also knew a period of growth under Charles Napier, who governed the island from 1822 to 1830. On July 1, 1823, Lord Byron visited the island. Byron was appointed representative and agent of the committee in Greece in a period of internal turmoil. He spent the first six weeks in Argostoli and then moved to Metaxata in Livathos because he said the environment was healthier and the scenery more beautiful.

After the death of Maitland in 1824, Frederic Adam was appointed to the post of governor; he was milder and more law-abiding than his predecessor, and took more interest in education; it was Adam who established the Ionian Academy.

In 1831 the philhellene Nuggent was appointed governor. He was in favour of constitutional reforms, but was not able to put them into practice. In 1835 he was succeeded by Baron Howard Douglas, who strengthened the bureaucracy and squandered public funds, arousing public opinion against him. Sir Stewart Mackenzie, who took over from him in 1841, was a supporter of agriculture and a patron of the arts. The next governor of the Ionian islands, John Seaton, affable and fair-minded, governed in a way beneficial to the islanders and instituted some constitutional reforms.

The 1830s saw the beginning of a more general reform. Young Kefalonians returning from Europe began to cultivate the idea of union with the rest of Greece. The liberals became extremely active, and England was forced to grant certain privileges, such as freedom of the press and establishment of a Parliament.

A black-and-white photograph of the English governor Napier, creator of the island's network of roads and its first public buildings (Korgialenio Museum)

The rock where the philhellene Lord Byron sat in Lakithra, with a dedication which does great honour to Greece

Drapano bridge, a work by de Bosset, caused waves of reaction because of the danger of enemy access to the capital in troubled times.
A pre-earthquake photograph of Argostoli bridge (Korgialenio Museum)

On September 14/26, 1848, the Kefalonians rebelled against the English, clashing with the English army at Drapano bridge in Argostoli; there was also fighting in Lixouri. Arrests, trials and jailings followed. Thus an unofficial crackdown on the liberals began, and three new parties were created, the Radicals, the Reformers and the Conservatives. Sir Henry George Ward was forced to restore freedom of the press and freedom to form organisations before the rebellion would simmer down.

Economic and social conditions in Kefalonia in 1849 were such that the movement found a response in the middle and lower classes. The class of signori was scandalised at the government's attitude, and claimed that it was not taking satisfactory measures to ensure public safety. They were coming to realise that it was freedom of the press that had mobilised the forces of the bourgeoisie. Their political and economic privileges were becoming endangered. With the political awakening of the people would come the demand for the restructuring of government on a more equitable basis.

The people did not hide their repugnance for the occupying forces, newspapers had no qualms about printing criticisms of the English, and it was not long before another revolt broke out, between August 15/27, in Skala. On September 2, Ward arrived on the island, quashed the rebellion and imposed martial law. The twenty-one instigators were executed by hanging, another 34 were jailed and 87 whipped.

In 1850, England approved the constitutional reforms and allowed the Ionian islands to freely elect 10 representatives to Parliament. The Radicals won the election. In mid-September, 1851, Ward returned to Argostoli, banned the islanders' organisations and exiled two leaders of the Radicals, thus winning the disapproval of the people for a second time. Ilias Zervos Iakovatos, editor of the "Fileleftheros" newspaper, and Iosif Momferatos, editor of "Anagenissis", were exiled to Kithira and Othoni respectively. Gerassimos Livadas, one of the pioneers of the radical movement who escaped arrest, voiced his opposition by sending memoranda to the English Parliament.

In 1858 when the British envoy W. E. Gladstone arrived in Kefalonia to carry out an enquiry into the government of the Ionian islands, he censured Ward for his tactics, but hardly did anything else.

Ward's successor, John Young, was more lenient. He allowed the exiled radicals to return in 1857, after popular demand in the Ionian Parliament. The next governor was Sir Henry Storks. In the elections of 1862, the popular vote went to the Radical Party and its leaders.

The Socialist Movement

At the beginning of August 1863 European diplomacy was once again occupied with the Septinsular question. Thus, as King Otto of Greece was being deposed, a protocol was being signed uniting the Ionian islands with Greece. King George I, son of the prince of Denmark, came to the throne of the newly-united country. Now that the much-hoped-for union had been achieved, the Ionian islands would in future share the fate of Greece, which at that time depended politically and economically on England. In June of 1864 the king visited Kefalonia.

The earthquake of January 23, 1867 struck mainly on the western side of the island, claiming 224 lives. Repeated earthquakes and infertile soil were among the driving forces of the great wave of emigration which began around the middle of the 19th century.

Trade unionism appeared early on the Ionian islands; unions were founded in the first few decades after unity with Greece. Some distinguished islanders who supported socialist ideas were P. Panas, R. Hoidas and M. Antipas from Kefalonia and P. Drakoulis from Ithaki. They were all instrumental in spreading socialist ideas to the rest of Greece. Panas and Hoidas prepared the way for Antipas; among his achievements was

The statue of the Socialist, Marinos Antipas, in Potamianata. He was imprisoned and murdered on March 9, 1907, because his ideas conflicted with the interests of the big landowners (G. Moustakis collection)

Doxology at the Church of the Saviour in Lithostroto (March 25, 1904, Korgialenio Museum, Argostoli)

the propagation of his socialist ideas to Thessaly, where the share-croppers in the plain revolted.

During World War I (1912-1913), Kefalonian women volunteered as nurses and cared for the wounded in hospitals. The Socialist Party's potential was differentiated in the years that followed, first by Eleftherios Venizelos, leader of the Liberals, and later by the Kefalonian Ioannis Metaxas, leader of the Free Thinkers and supporter of the Royalists. The expulsion of the democrats from Kefalonia pales before the greater danger of the war which began on October 28, 1940.

On April 6, 1941, Hitler attacked Greece for the first time and united his forces with those of the Italians. On June 11, 1943, the Italians surrendered to the Allies and on September 8, the Germans took Rome. The German occupation in Kefalonia began on September 24, 1943. Nazi brutality reach a climax in the mass slaughter of officers of the Acqui Division. The prisoners of war, who had surrendered without resistance, were led to the "Red Villa" and from there to a cave higher up, where they were executed. The Nazi occupation lasted only a year, but it was a bitter ordeal for the indomitable people of Kefalonia. The majority of the islanders joined the organised national resistance movement. Lootings, arrests and executions were daily occurrences. The German occupation forces finally left the island on September 10, 1944.

A series of earthquakes between August 9 and 12, 1953 left the islands of Kefalonia and Ithaki in ruins. Of course, there had in the past been other earthquakes not mentioned here, but they had claimed relatively fewer victims and caused less material damage.

Italian troops raising their flag in the main square of Argostoli ("I martiri de Cefalonia" by Don Luigi Chilardini, Milan, 1925)

"Athinaiki", August 12, 1953: "This earthquake produced energy equal to 1,750,000,000 KwH, roughly the equivalent of 63 atom bombs."

"To Vima", August 11, 1953: "The first seismic shock occurred in Vathi, capital of Ithaki at 9:40 am, when most people were inside their houses."

"Eleftheria", August 11, 1953: "The earthquake which occurred at 9:41 am and lasted for 33 seconds caused the most damage in Ithaki. The Nomarch of Kefalonia reports that in the capital of Ithaki, Vathi, over 200 houses were rendered uninhabitable and 20 collapsed."

*"Ta Nea" – No. 71, August 12, 1953: "
A terrible earthquake which occurred at 11:27 today and lasted for 50 seconds completely destroyed the town of Argostoli. The news was transmitted by the munitions carrier "Alfios" which was in the territorial waters of Kefalonia."*

"Paris Match", August, 22/29 1953: "Argostoli, capital of Kefalonia, has been razed. Between August 9 and 14, 113 seismic tremors reduced the island's 350 towns and villages to dust."

*Beta S. Galiatsatou wrote in her book "During the Hours of the Earthquakes in Kefalonia":
"The Ghost Town:
...And later, when we had recovered somewhat from the first tragic impression and took a dazed look around us, there was nothing left of what had formerly been. Enceladus had arrived, a self-invited companion, to play his role on the stage of our lives. And this strange set designer changed all the scenery around us, turning our homes into ruins. He played the part of an eccentric architect, who with a single movement changed the old style of our houses, because that was the way he wanted it to be. We looked but we couldn't believe our eyes! Ruins! Ruins everywhere! And in the distance stood the mountains which up until now had been hidden by our houses! But what spectacle did the people present? Was it perhaps hell with living people hidden inside it? They were people, but somehow they looked like something else. The dust had formed entire masks over their faces, and all that showed was two eyes big from horror, and lips so dry and pale that you would think that life had left them long ago. Their bodies covered by half-torn clothes, they looked like dead bodies that had just been thrown from their graves, and without knowing what they wanted in this place they had found themselves in, they looked curiously at the demolished houses.
Perhaps Dante would not have called on Virgil to be his imaginary companion in writing his famous Inferno, if he had lived for a short time during these moments in Argostoli.
Moments of unbalance and madness...."*

A Kefalonian peasant of the 19th century ("Kefaliniaka", Vol. I, Costumes 1953, collection of K. P. Fokas Kosmetatos)

Folklore – Arts and Letters – Tradition

We could not fail to make at least a passing reference to the arts, since the Kefalonians have always been a cultured people with a thirst for knowledge. During the time when the rest of Greece was groaning under the Turkish yoke, Kefalonia was governed by the civilised city of Venice. The island's various conquerers brought with them their language, arts, style of dress, even their habits and customs. Naturally, progressive Kefalonians copied some of this, after so many years of occupation by and co-habitation with one European or another, but they were never guilty of blind imitation. The free and innovative spirit of the islanders took foreign influences and made them a starting-point for creativity. Consider the Kefalonian's personality: foreign influence made him disobedient, revolutionary, impetuous and diplomatic. Even so, he remained witty, artistic and wily, like his ancestor, Odysseus. An experienced sailor, he plies the seas and visits beautiful lands, but remains forever nostalgic for his fatherland.

Intellectual communication with the rest of Europe helped numerous men of intellect make their mark. An important contributing factor to this intellectual flowering was the systematic education of wealthy Kefalonians in Western universities. Important authors, poets and composers gave the world superb works. From 1849 on, Argostoli began to gave birth to weekly newspapers, periodicals and satirical publications, most of which are still preserved in the Korgialeneios Library and various libraries in Athens.

Foreign influence first made itself felt in the language of the people. Foreign words, mainly Italian, came into use in everyday spoken language, either unchanged or blended with their Greek equivalents. In a short time, certain foreign habits were adopted. For example, the ruling class obliged young girls to study languages and take piano lessons; they drank tea in the afternoon and frequented the theatre. From their constant voyages to other countries, sailors brought home European lace, dresses, furniture and ornaments.

Diana Antonakatou has this to say on the subject of dress in Kefalonia:

"...A hundred women! Standing close together, they would not fill even one eighth of the space on Argostoli bridge, even though between the first and the last of them lie three thousand one hundred years or so, the whole arc described by the history of cloth-making through the centuries from Penelope's gown to the mini-dress of her last descendant. A hundred costumes that could dress the cho-

rus of a historical tragedy: Mycenean noblewomen, maids of Tanagra, young girls of the Classical era, Hellenistic ladies, aristocratic women of Rome, Byzantine wives and Frankish and Sicilian and Venetian and French and English ladies. The whole parade of influence on female dress: the whole tumultuous historical life of the island and its effect on the aspect of its women."

Of course, foreign influence in Kefalonia had its advantages, because it released women from quite a bit of drudgery and gave them a place in society not enjoyed by women in other parts of Greece at that time.

Kefalonia has a grand tradition in the area of the theatre. The first plays in Kefalonia, and in the other Ionian islands, were performed by touring Italian companies. By the beginning of the 19th century Greek-speaking companies had come into being. Their productions were poorly organised and more frugal, but they evoked a greater response from audiences. By that time it had become necessary to build a theatre. S. Berettas established the first theatre in Argostoli in 1805; despite the fact that it was built of wood, it was fully equipped. (Similar wooden theatres were common in the Italian countryside.) In 1823, Neofitos Vamvas, a clergyman, teacher and revolutionary, began to give lessons in dramatics, producing ancient Greek dramas in the ancient Greek language! Later, in 1837-1856, A. Solomos converted his Argostoli mansion into the island's the first real theatre building. Plays were also performed in other places, including halls in mansions and warehouses. Theatrical activity reached a pitch of intensity in 1830. Theatrical productions acquired a permanent home in 1857, with the inauguration of the Kefalos Theatre whose first production was Verdi's La Traviata. The desire to create a theatre had been so great that in order to obtain one a peculiar charter had been drawn up, according to which each one of the owners had his own box which he painted, furnished and rented as he wished, paying a certain sum to the theatre's common treasury. In the beginning, theatrical

An ebony secretaire fashioned in India, belonging to Ferdinand Lesseps and a mannequin wearing an evening gown (Korgialenio Museum)

A pair of opera glasses, 18th-century Venetian wallpaper, a silver bracelet, a silk scarf and an ivory fan (Korgialenio Museum)

A theatrical production in Agia Efimia (Moustakis collection)

companies were made up entirely of men, but it was not long before women, too, took their place on the boards. Plays were put on by Italian companies, Kefalonian amateurs and amateur players from other islands. Nor was all the activity confined to Argostoli. Lixouri did not build its own theatre, but plays were given in drawing-rooms of mansions, in the Xidias warehouse and in a large room in the Town Hall.

Around 1860, amateur friends of the theatre founded the Society of Friends of the Drama, whose goal was to produce plays by Kefalonian authors. Naturally, the islanders responded in the anticipated manner, and soon enthusiastic amateurs as well as authors and journalists were producing comedies, love stories, adventures, patriotic plays, etc.

In a 1903 issue of the satirical newspaper "Zizanion", there is an account of a performance in the Kefalos Theatre in Argostoli which ended in cat-calls:

"...in these explosive conditions the performance began on Carnival Sunday with "The Barber of Seville". The theatre was packed! People from Livathos, the cream of Argostoli society in the boxes, wearing their costly dresses and jewels. The foreign functionaries, the guests of the aristocracy, sitting near them!... The well-to-do bourgeois in the stalls ...and the gallery full of the labouring masses, bent from life's anxieties, the popolo..."

Music has always played a prominent role in Kefalonian life. In 582 BC at the 48th Olympic Games, the Kefalonian Melampus took a prize for the best musical composition. At the beginning of the 17th century, the whole of Europe, including music-loving Kefalonia, was under the influence of Italian music. In music, first place goes to Lixouri; according to the founder of the National School of Music, D. Lavrangas (1864-1941) it was there that the arietta came into being. This term is perhaps a variation of the Italian a orecchia (by ear), that is, a song sung according to how the singers conceive it, as the musicologist S. A. Skiadaressis explains. Ariettas slowly developed into entirely Greek creations. The people themselves became composer and creator, improvising both words and music. This type of song is sung by three, four or more rarely five singers, usually simple fishermen. One begins to sing and at the right moment the others join in. This type of music is sung without any instrumental accompaniment.

Serenades are local folk songs which, unlike ariettas, must be accompanied by a guitar, even if the guitarist doesn't always know how to play! The rest of the company sings in harmony with the lead singer. In the serenade, as in most genuine songs of the people, their hopes and the social conditions in which they live are always reflected. There were also love songs and jocular couplets, written by the singers themselves to express disappointment in love.

On May 8, 1838, a group of anonymous young music-lovers circulated a document soliciting donations from the inhabitants of Argostoli with a view to establishing a Philharmonic School. Generous contributions poured in, and the creation of the Argostoli Philharmonic in 1842 and the Pale Philharmonic in Lixouri in 1836 made musical studies available to broader social strata.

The art of chanting in Kefalonia differs from ecclesiastical music in the rest of Greece. In the beginning it was based on Byzantine tradition. Later other Byzantine hymns were absorbed following the great wave of immigration from Crete. The result was a style of chanting of a purely Kefalonian stamp, full of harmony and grandeur.

The dance has always been an element of popular expression, a display of a frame of mind, interpreted in steps and movement. Formal balls were given by the Venetians and wealthy islanders. It was in the class of small merchants that popular public dances had their beginnings; they, too, were the privilege of a certain class at first. In time dancing schools and dance halls made their appearance.

The dance was always closely connected with music. The Lyceum of Greek Girls performing traditional dances outside the Argostoli Philharmonic School

Local folk dances were influenced by Cretan as well as Peloponnesian dancing. They soon took on a character all their own. In former times dances were usually accompanied by voices without instruments, and if there were any instruments, they were shepherds' pipes or, later, violins, guitars or mandolins. The two people at the head of the line in these dances hold a handerchief between them, so that the lead dancer can perform figures. Many of these

Comic figures preparing to burn the remains of the Carnival (Lixouri, February 26, 1960, G. Galanos collection)

dances are still very much alive, and are performed at festivals in the countryside, held to celebrate the feast-day of a saint or during Carnival season.

Carnival in Kefalonia is celebrated with special brilliance, impressive costumes and masks. It is a holiday imported from Venice with a long tradition behind it. In former times, groups of eight couples danced cadrilles, lancers and pole-dances in the town squares. The appearance of the masqueraders was also striking at the celebrations on the first Monday in Lent, held in the countryside; they always provided a good opportunity for public satire, particularly at the time when the press did not yet exist. Sometimes, if groups of opponents happened to be present, a "duel in verse" would start up and last for hours!

Architecture on the island was influenced by the Renaissance and Baroque. It was greatly simplified, preserving only the basic elements of those styles. The homes of the people had their origins in the necessities of peasant life, but in the end took on a petty bourgeois form. Their exterior was reminiscent of the architecture of central Greece, but rooms were larger and outside stairs were made of stone. The islanders also a precocious awareness of the need for toilets. Interiors were decorated with furniture and other objects brought to Kefalonia by Greek and foreign sailors; many such unique pieces are on exhibit in the Korgialeneio Historical and Folklore Museum in Argostoli. The 1953 earthquakes destroyed mansions at a time when the rest of Greece was still living in wooden huts. Many factors contributed to this, among them imitation of the homes of the foreign and Greek bourgeoisie and the wealth the island's sailors brought home with them. Unfortunately, only a few remnants of that era can be seen today, among them

An impressive pre-earthquake door in the village of Domata

"Psyche", a work of the famous sculptor Bonanos (Drapano public cemetery, Argostoli)

houses, churches and bell-towers; most of them lie in ruins in small villages, untouched since the day they fell.

Sculpture was developed on the island, particularly during the 16th century. Carved altar-screens and iconostases from that era still adorn the island's churches and monasteries. Some examples of such ecclesiastical art are on exhibit in the Korgialeneio Museum in Argostoli. One of Kefalonia's well-known sculptors is G. Bonanos (1863-1939). Representative examples of his work may be seen in the English and Greek cemeteries in Drapano and Lixouri.

The art of painting in Kefalonia is no less significant; it evolved during the 16th and 17th centuries and can be encountered mainly in icons. Icon-painting on the island was influenced chiefly by the Cretan artists, who were driven from their island by the Turks; their influence was rounded out with Italian elements. Many icons taken from churches destroyed in earthquakes are housed in the Korgialeneio Museum, the Ecclesiastical Museum of Apostolos Andreas and the Tipaldon-Iakovaton Public Library and Museum in Lixouri.

Konstantinos Tipaldos-Iakovatos, Metropolitan of Stavroupolis and professor at the Ionian Academy (Tipaldon-Iakovaton Museum, Lixouri)

Altar-screen from the church of Agios Georgios, owned by Z. Horafas, in Lixouri (Korgialenio Museum)

The seaside road in Argostoli. At the left, the Church of Sissiotissa. The seaside buildings are reflected in

Argostoli

Argostoli, built on the western side of a natural harbour surrounded by mountains, is suggestive of a Norwegian fjord. Its geographical location is considered a privileged one because it boasts both surface and underground water. In 1555

vater of Koutavos lagoon

the springs of Koutavos were first used; before that Koutavos was a vast expanse of marshy land. Farther back in time, when Argostoli was an anchorage for Turkish raiders and pirates, water was obtained from two wells dug during the stay of the formidable pirate Barbarossa.

Up until the early 14th century this

area was a desolate, rocky expanse known as Peskaria (or Psaroskala or Psaradika). In 1560 a makeshift dock was built so that passengers could disembark. What is today the town then consisted of a few fishermen's cottages, smugglers' dens and the chapel of Ai-Nikolas, surrounded by fields and vineyards. Raisin production in the mid-14th century drew ships of various nationalities to Kefalonia. When the island was finally purged of pirates, trade and shipping began to thrive. But the authorities installed in the fortress could not exercise the necessary degree of control, to the detriment of the island's economy. This need for control, as well as what was at that time a great distance between the Agios Georgios fortress and the harbour (4 km.), led to the building of warehouses for commercial use. By 1632 the fortress contained living quarters, prisons and shops, and quarantine facilities were added in 1705.

As S. Marinatos has observed, Kefalonia is one of the few places in Greece with such a large proportion of ancient place-names. This shows that its population remained unmixed. Regarding the more modern, often peculiar place-names to be met with, the explanation is given by the Academician K. Amantos: in medieval Greece, names of places and land were taken from the their founder or owner, for example, the surname Metaxas became Metaxata, Domos became Domata, Kourkoumelis became Kourkoumelata. As far as Cretan surnames and place-names are concerned, Marinatos wrote in the Belgian review "Byzantium" in 1935 that they are so numerous on the island that Kefalonia might better be called Little Crete. In "Neon Ellinomnimona" by S. Lambrou there is a list of the Cretan families of Corfu who emigrated to the Ionian islands during the 16th century. Among the Kefalonian surnames listed there is the surname Argostolis. Perhaps it predated the Cretans, though, because it is also mentioned in tax lists for fish-hatchery rentals in 1579.

In the 16th century, all-powerful Venice began to go into decline. In 1753 the island's notables sent Ioannis Dellaportas to Venice to ask that Argostoli be made administrative centre, and in 1755 the general purveyor Sagredos petitioned to the same purpose. Finally, in 1759, Argostoli became the capital of the island.

Argostoli was also the island's administrative and commercial centre. By 1800 it had evolved into a elegant, genteel provincial town, with stone-paved streets and a orderly street-plan. The wooden huts had given way to imposing mansions, churches and nine tall bell-towers. In 1908 the town was electrified.

R. Mavromihali, in her book "Kithnos and Kefalonia – My Blue Travels", writes on the houses of Argostoli before the earthquakes:

"...houses were built in the «Kefalonian» style. The craftsmen (master builders) took elements from Venetian Baroque, adding some of their own from Kefalonian folk art. They applied their own personal inspiration..."

...Interiors of the houses were almost always painted in two colours. The Kefalonians showed excellent taste in decorating the insides of their homes. The wealthy were accustomed to importing Venetian, English (Regency) or French (Louis Philippe) furniture. A lot was left behind by the successive conquerors when they left, and the islanders either bought it or ransacked their houses..."

...Even in the houses of the poor one could find fine furniture, together with the simple furniture of the people. Someone in the family had been a traveller or some Frank had «thrown it away»..."

All these things were completely destroyed in the earthquake of August

The main square in Argostoli – the centre of morning and evening life in the town. On the left, the statue of the town's benefactor, Vallianos

12, 1953. With the help of the government and the astonishing private initiative of the islanders, the town was rebuilt immediately. Present-day Argostoli is no longer the romantic provincial town of the 18th century, but it is nevertheless a charming, modern town trying to preserve its former appearance in lovely neo-classical churches and other buildings. In Argostoli's main square, which is lined with restaurants and coffee-bars, stands the statue of one of the town's benefactors, Vallianos. To the left of it are the offices of the Nomarch and opposite them the beautiful buildings of the Bank of Greece and the Museum of the P.F. Kosmetatos Foundation, not at present open to the public.

Also well worth a visit is the Archaeological Museum, behind the Prefect's

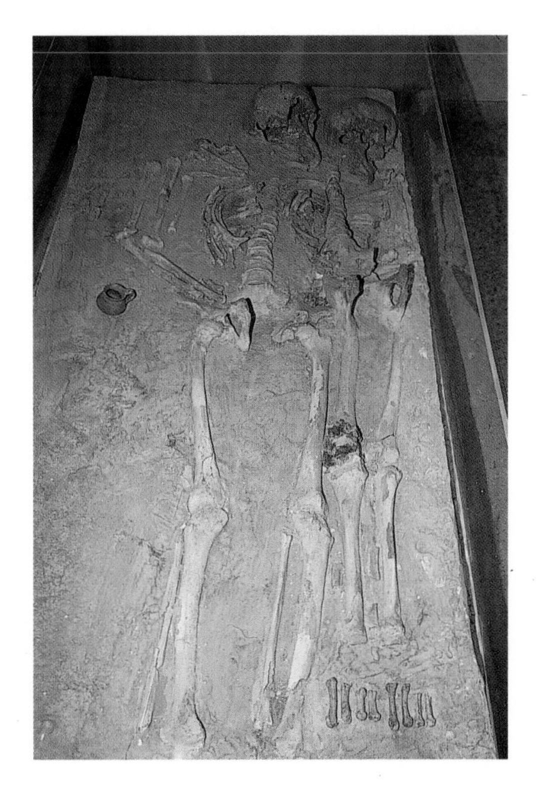

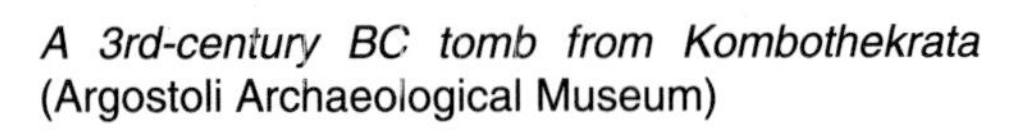

A 3rd-century BC tomb from Kombothekrata (Argostoli Archaeological Museum)

offices. Certain to catch visitors' attention on their right as they enter the Museum is a 3rd-century BC grave from Kombothekrata, which contains a male and a female skeleton and grave goods. The Museum's three rooms house burial items from the island's graves and finds from the Mycenean, Hellenistic and Roman periods, including pottery, tools, jewelry, coins, a Roman mosaic, etc.).

Above the Archaeological Museum, the restoration of the Kefalos Theatre, which operated from 1857 to 1907, is now nearing completion. Some fine Italian melodramas were performed in this historic theatre by Italian and Greek actors. In the beginning it was run on funds collected from private individuals; later it was financed by the local government, and after union with Greece by the municipality. We might note here that the art-loving inhabitants of Argostoli saw to it that they had a theatre even before they had a hospital! In 1922 the Kefalos Theatre was used as living quarters for refugees from Asia Minor, and during World War II it was ignited by German aircraft fire and burned down. Its destruction was completed by the earthquakes in 1953.

Above the Theatre the road leads to the Korgialeneios Library of Argostoli, one of the largest in Greece, with 46,000 volumes and a small concert hall. It was built in 1924 with a legacy left by Marinos Korgialeneios.

On its ground floor is the splendid Korgialeneio Historical and Folklore Museum. A visit to it will take you back to Argostoli before the earthquakes. In its five rooms, you will see collections of old lace and embroidery, clothes worn by members of the island's high society, furniture, maps and photographs before and

Vintage gown, paintings, musical instruments, embroidery, ladies' accessories and two mannequins wearing Kefalonian costumes (Korgialenio Historical and Folklore Museum, Argostoli)

The Gentilinis-Kosmetatos home in old Dikastirion Avenue (Korgialenio Museum). *Only the first story of this building was left standing after the 1953 earthquakes, but it is a reminder of an age gone by*

after the earthquake, reconstructions of rooms, ecclesiastical items, and peasants' utensils and tools.

In front of the Archaeological Museum a road begins which leads to Lithostroto – the heart of the marketplace since the time when elegant shoppers bought hats, patent-leather shoes and Bohemian crystal. Today you can buy souvenirs from the tourist shops there. Lithostroto was the first section of town to be built and inhabited immediately. Angelos-Dionissis Dembonos tells us that Agios Vassilis (Santa Claus's Greek counterpart) came to Argostoli from Lithostroto! Here we find the Church of Agios Spiridon, with a carved and gilded wooden altar-screen. The Church is the starting-point for the procession commemorating the 1953 earthquakes held each year on August 12, in which the municipal band participates. On the same street stands the Roman Catholic Church of Agios Nikolaos.

Out of the town's nine bell-towers existing before the earthquakes, only the clock tower of the Church of Theotokos Rakatzis has been rebuilt. It was originally built in 1843 by the Horafas family. A side-street on the right takes us to the front of the Cathedral or Metropolis, built in 1957 (Evangelistria, Analipsi, Agios Georgios); a little farther up is the Metropolitan's residence. In Vergoti Street there is an art gallery.

From the square another wide road begins which leads to the southern part of the island. On it you will encounter the "Spiti tou Daskalou" – a ground-floor exhibition hall – and the Philharmonic School. Historians are divided on the question of when the latter was founded. I. Tsitselis believes that it was created in 1836, but D. Lavrangas sets the date as sometime after 1842. Opposite it stands

The Catholic Church of Agios Nikolaos with its bell-tower, in Lithostroto

The Agii Theodori lighthouse, a work by Napier, offers one of the best sunsets on the island

the Kosmetatos house, whose first floor is part of the original building existing before the earthquake. The little Church of Agia Anni is tucked away in a side-street on the left. A little farther on we find the old Church of the Archangeli dating from 1906.

The road to Livathos from Argostoli passes Farao hill, the best place to get a photograph of the whole town. The chapel of Agios Athanassios on the hill above Argostoli commands another striking view, of the Lassi peninsula, Vardiani islet and Lixouri bay.

From the seaside road, an uphill turnoff makes the round of Lassi peninsula. A twenty-minute walk through wildflowers and thyme will take you to the monument dedicated to the fallen Italians; from here there is a panoramic view. Now the downhill road is effortless; it will take you past the Italians' hiding-place to the house where the Germans held them until they executed them.

At the far end of the beach stands the Agii Theodori lighthouse, built in 1829,

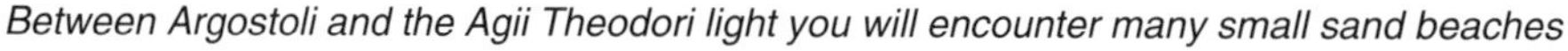

Between Argostoli and the Agii Theodori light you will encounter many small sand beaches

Katavothres may no longer be a mystery to mankind, but it is one of the favourite evening haunts of visitors to the island

yet another work of the British governor Napier. It is a round Doric building encircled by columns 3.6 m in height. It was destroyed in the 1875 earthquake and rebuilt on its original plans. If you happen to come here in the evening, you will enjoy one of the island's best sunsets!

The road continues along the coast, passing the Argostoli camping grounds. Those staying in Argostoli can make use of the small beaches that stretch from the campsite to the Agii Theodori lighthouse. On the way back to Argostoli you will encounter one of Kefalonia's strangest phenomena, the Katavothres. Tremendous quantities of sea-water pour into them continually, without returning; their depth and magnitude are unknown. The pine-clad area boasts tavernas, discotheques and nightclubs.

The lower level of the water here (about 1.3 m lower than the rest of the sea) and its entry into the Katavothres were first observed in 1835 by the astonished citizens of Argostoli. Before the Second World War, the islanders exploited this difference in level by placing a 5-8 HP mill there to generate electricity.

Many researchers have tried to determine where the water which flows in at the Katavothres flows out again. Over the years they used various materials and dyes, such as oil, petroleum, sawdust, etc. These efforts produced no result until on February 26, 1963 G. Petrohilos and Austrian geologists threw in 140 kg. of uranin, a water-soluble dye in powder form. It was 14 days before the first faint traces of green appeared in the villages of Karavomilos, Fridi and Agia Efimia and in Melissani Lake. The mill now houses small lobster hatcheries.

At night the town puts on its jewels and beckons visitors to relax and enjoy themselves. Drapano bridge today

The obelisk on Drapano bridge bearing the name of de Bosset and an inscription in four languages dedicated to the English

One relic of old Argostoli that survived the earthquakes is Drapano bridge with its characteristic arches. It is of English construction; it spanned the wide harbour of Argostoli and ensured direct communication with most of the island's more densely populated areas. It also formed a capacious fish-hatchery, which separated Koutavos lagoon from the harbour. The obelisk that stands in the middle of the bridge commemorates the construction date (1813) and the person who inspired it, Colonel de Bosset. Like every great work, the building of the bridge touched

›rovides visitors from the surrounding villages with a link to Argostoli

off opposition in the government council. Objections to it included fear of attack from the island's other villages, financial difficulties, possible danger of infection from the lagoon, even the fact that its some of its supports would be over 5 m deep. Finally the original wooden bridge was built, which was replaced four years later by stone arches. Thirty years later it was rebuilt of stone.

The Church of Panagia Sissiotissa stands at its entrance. The harbour jetty's pebble pavement and palm-trees make it the best place for an evening stroll. Lin-

As soon as night begins to fall, the seaside promenade becomes the starting point from which visitors to Argostoli set out for an evening of fun.

The bell-tower of the Church of Agia Varvara; from it one can see the whole town

ing it are most of the shops one will need for his daily purchases.

A turnoff to the right climbs the small hill to the Mili locale, whose main attraction is a ruined mill. Lean over the small bridge a little farther on, to see the chapel of Agia Varvara below, whose chancel is built into the rock.

Continue on the main road from Argostoli to Sami. The villages of Potamiana produce the famous Rombola wine. It is truly a wonder how the inhabitants of these villages managed to tame the barren, arid land and grow such fine grapes.

A short detour to the left from Agia Varvara leads to **Prokopata**, with its labyrinthine streets; it was built after the earthquake with money donated by the shipowner P. Markessinis. The next village you come to on the main road is **Faraklata**, which stands on a hill. The people in this area can foresee the sex of an unborn child by examining the belly-button of the family's youngest member. If it faces upward, the baby will be a boy; if it faces downward, it will be a girl.

Back on the main road, go on for another 7 km until you come to **Dilinata**. On the hill opposite stands the Church of Panagia Lamia, built in the Septinsular architectural style; its bell-tower has fallen. The island's churches and monasteries are surely well worth a visit; however you may find some of them locked, out of fear of burglars. Don't despair! Apply to the president of the village, or to the nearest house, and someone will be happy to let you in and show you around.

The road which goes straight on from the bridge towards Lixouri passes in front of a wooded area which leads to the Drapano cemetery; its monuments date back as far as 1848. Macabre as the idea might seem, some of the monuments are not to be missed, among them "Psyche" (381), that of Angeliki Lomverdou and the sarcophagus on the right-hand side of the cemetery church.

On the main road from Argostoli to Sami you will come to **Razata**, which offers a few rooms to rent. A passable dirt road to the right of the main road winds up in the ancient city of **Crane** (Paleokastro), one of the island's four ancient cities. It took its name either from the son of Cephalus, Cranius, or from the Cornel Tree (Krania), from which the ancient inhabitants made their bows. The

Filipotis' "Sleeper" and the bell-tower of Drapaniotissa (Drapano Public Cemetery)

bow that Artemis gave to Procris, which later caused her death, was made of the wood of the Cornel Tree.

Still standing are the Cyclopean walls built of huge stone blocks dating from the 7th century BC; they are one of the best examples of the art of fortification from that era. Remains of a Doric temple of Demeter can also be seen. A little farther up stands the chapel of Agia Varvara (Agios Varvaros), in a cave. The rectangular cavern hollowed out of the rock near the top of the hill is known as Drakospilia. It was most probably a Hellenistic or Roman tomb of a wealthy person. A little further down, at the site of Ai-Grigoris, the archaeologist Marinatos excavated a series of tombs from the 5th century BC. The necropolis of Crane lay on the south side of the hill, at the Riza locale. The cube-shaped rock tombs found there had all been looted and destroyed.

It would seem that the ancient inhabitants never cremated their dead. They laid them on their backs with their legs crossed in graves which they filled in with earth and stones. (In the rest of Greece they were merely placed on the floor.) Some of the graves had been emptied and used again for other burials. There were, however, instances where other family members were buried on top of the first corpse.

An inscribed tiered base with a dedication to Demeter and Kore from the Doric temple of Demeter in ancient Crane (Argostoli Archaeological Museum)

The 7th-century BC Cyclopean walls of ancient Crane, one of the best examples of the art of fortification from that era

The famous, vast beach of Makris Gialos and Platis Gialos, ideal for every kind of water sport

Argostoli – Monastery of Apostolos Andreas – Fortress of Agios Georgios

Using Argostoli as a base, you can tour the island's villages. The area you will visit first is known as Giros tis Livathos – drenched in vegetation, its villages are among the island's most wealthy; it boasts well-tended gardens, famous churches and lovely beaches. There are two roads leading to it. One is the coast road, which first passes a thick pine forest and the small Bay of Kalamia. A narrow cement-paved road from the **Spilia** locale leads to a small chapel and to the cave of Agios Gerassimos, where the saint lived as a hermit for six years before he settled in Omala valley. Those who prefer developed beaches and water sports will have the opportunity to visit the excellent string of beaches of Makris Gialos, Platis Gialos and Tourkopodaro. It was here that in 1537 the brave Kefalonian woman, Diatsenta of Vardesseras, threw herself into the sea rather than be ravished by the pirate Barbarossa. This area has evolved into a tourist resort in recent years; it boasts the island's best beaches and biggest hotel complexes, and of course a vibrant night-life.

You will pass through **Minies**, the village that had to relocate twice due to Barbarossa's raids. Now it stands above the plain and is known for the ruins of a 6th-century BC Doric temple, as well as

Tourkopodaro, at the end of Makris Gialos and Platis Gialos beaches

the Church of Theotokos Mangana dating from 1666. The Virgin Mary, to which the church is dedicated, is said to have freed a monk the pirates had bound in chains. These chains are still hanging on the throne of the icon to commemorate the miracle. The church's altar-screen was undamaged in the earthquakes. The village of **Sarlata** was once the home of the Livathos Philharmonic. The locals tell an old story about the stone slab covering a grave in the Church: It belongs to Captain Fokas, a dashing, bold sailor, who ran into a storm and was forced to land in Turkish-dominated Crete. Near a spring he met the daughter of the Bey of Crete and fell madly in love with her. His feelings were reciprocated, she left her father and his palace, was baptised Ekaterini and married her true love.

From there the road ascends to **Svoronata**, overlooked by the imposing bell-tower of Agios Nikolaos and an old mill on the hill. On the far side of the village is Avithos beach, which has something of the aura of a moonscape: a bare rock surrounded by red sand, which is carried away in winter by sea currents, only to be brought back again in summer.

A half-mile offshore is Dias islet, which may have taken its name from an altar to Zeus (Dias) which once stood there, or from the Cretan islet of Dias. The priests here synchronised their sacrifices with those at the temple of Aenesian Zeus on the peak of Mt. Ainos. The islet was used

Avithos beach with its red sand

as a place of exile for members of the clergy during the time of the English occupation. A hundred steps lead up from the small jetty to the chapel of Panagia Vlahernon, founded by a hermit; it celebrates its feast-day on July 2. The chapel was demolished in the 1953 earthquake and rebuilt by I. Vallianos. Next to Dias is another rocky islet, Mizithris.

The façade and the altar-screen of the Church of the Panagia in Domata

In **Domata** (formerly Sklavata, due to the existence of slaves (sklavos), don't miss the Church of the Panagia with a marvellous carved and gilded wooden altar-screen dating from the 19th century. Its gilt was obtained by melting down 12,000 gold sovereigns. Housed here is the makeshift coffin in which Captain M. Sklavos transported the remains of the Patriarch Gregorius V from the Bosporus to Odessa. Near Domata stands one of

the island's huge old olive-trees, which may be thousands of years old. The locals call it the "chatting olive". Ten to twenty people can sit inside its hollow trunk, and it takes that many to stretch their arms around it. A good place to swim is Ai-Heli beach with its dark sand.

In **Kalligata** there is another finely-carved baroque altar-screen in the 18th-century Church of the Panagia.

The village of **Kourkoumelata** was inhabited as far back as 1490 BC. Today's village, rebuilt by the island's great benefactor G. Vergotis after the earthquakes, is modern, with a well-conceived street-plan. Its houses are not built in the Kefalonian style, since it was modeled on a Swiss country town, but its inhabitants are especially proud of the Stadium and the Neoclassical building housing the Cultural Center.

Metaxata was the seat of the archbishopric of Cephallenia after the Eastern church was reinstated; until the middle of the 15th century the island had Latin bishops. The villagers of Metaxata were the first to introduce printing to Greece. Opposite the Church of Agia Paraskevi stands a white house on the site of a house where Lord Byron once stayed. Napier writes in his journal:

"...To the admirers of Lord Byron, the village is a holy place, because he lived here for three months before departing to Messolongi and to his death (1823-24).

Pottery from the excavations in 1960 in Metaxata (Argostoli Archaeological Museum)

As I did not speak Greek, I had some difficulty in finding the house, because, as I later discovered, he was known to the inhabitants only as «Milord».

The house is small but it stands in one of the most isolated corners of this lovely village, with a wonderful view of the rich plain on one side and of the Castle of Agios Georgios and Mt. Ainos on the other..."

"...Count Gamba complained bitterly about his eccentricities, pointing out that he was often unbearable after midnight and that the phases of the moon undoubtedly had an effect on him..."

Just below the church, in the vicinity of Halikera, Professor Marinatos discovered three Mycenean chamber tombs in 1933-1934.

Lakithra, capital of Livathos since 1887, was rebuilt by the French. The archaeologist A. Goekoop believed this

The Church of Agios Gerassimos and the Neoclassical building which houses the Cultural Centre in Kourkoumelata, a gift of the island's great benefactor G. Vergotis

to be the site of Odysseus' city; more specifically, he thought it was located where the Church of Agios Nikolaos ton Aliprantidon stands today, in the vicinity of Kallithea, where Lord Byron sat on a rock and had the inspriation for one of his poems. Near the Church four late Mycenean tombs of 1250-1150 BC were found, full of pottery and other artefacts. Of the 400 clay vessels found, 300 have been pieced together. Musical groups and choirs have been appearing at the Kallithea club on the top of the hill ever since the 1930s. A great celebration takes place in this area on the feast-day of Agia Anna.

The **Monastery of Apostolos Andreas** is one of the five monasteries that once existed in the area. It dates back to Byzantine times, with tombs from the 6th and 7th centuries. It was originally dedicated to Panagia Milapidia (apple-pear), because an icon of the Virgin was found on the lifeless trunk of such a tree. In a document of 1264 it is referred to for the first time by the name of Apostolos Andreas. Its church has suffered much damage in earthquakes, and was rebuilt twice, in 1587 and in 1953. After 1953 it was converted into an ecclesiastical museum and next to it a basilica of Panagia Milapidia was built. This church houses the sole of the right foot of the Apostle Andrew. It is believed to have been donated to the monastery in the 17th century by Princess Roxanne (the nun Romyla), daughter of the titled Epirote Tsigaras.

In the superb museum in the old church you will see fine 13th-century frescos in the chancel, and more recent ones, dating from the 17th and 18th centuries, on the side walls. The altar-screen dates from 1612. To its left is the icon of Panagia Milapidia. The frescos from the Church of the Taxiarhi, now in ruins, have been removed, transferred to canvas and brought here to the museum. The muse-

Goekoop placed Odysseus' city near the Church of Agios Nikolaos ton Aliprantidon. Many years later, Lord Byron wrote some of his poems sitting on a rock on the same site.
From Grave I in Lakithra a small crater from the Mycenean era now in the Archaeological Museum

um's icons represent the work of several famous artists over a period of centuries. One of them is the priceless icon of Panagia Akathistos (1700), painted in the Byzantine-Italian style by the Cretan icon-painter papa-Stefanos Tsankarolos. Also housed here are the shroud of the Patriarch Gregorius V, relics of saints, hand-written letters of Cosmas the Aetolian, bishops' vestments, etc. (Opening hours 9 am-1 pm and 5 pm-8 pm)

On the other side of the main road is **Keramies**. A handsome mansion with Doric columns graces the road leading to this very ancient village. Keramies was the birthplace of the benefactor P. Vallianos, scion of a bold, enterprising family of grain merchants and shipowners. The family's graves can be seen in the cemetery dating from 1903. In the town square with the small fountain stand the fine church of Agios Vassilios, built in the Russian style, and superb traditional mansions, with intricate ornamentation of wood and plaster. A little farther down are the old earthquake-proof homes of the Vallianos family. The same road passes through **Spartia**, an old village mentioned in the records of the Latin Bishopric of Cephallenia in 1264. In order to repel attacks by Saracen pirates, the village's narrow streets were laid out in a maze-like pattern. The courtyards of the houses are surrounded by high walls with tiny windows. This was the birthplace of V. Panas, a member of the Friendly Society of Greek patriots and commander of the Kefalonians in the battle of Lalas against the Turks. At the middle of the 19th century the fleet of Spartia comprised 90 sailing vessels which carried commercial goods throughout the Mediterranean and the Black Sea. The small Church of Agios Gerassimos still has its bell-tower dating from 1400. The Church of the Panagia used to preserve the bed of

Precipitous white rocks shelter the small harbour and beach in Spartia

Pessada beach has shallow water suitable for children

Cosmas the Aetolian; it was carried in a procession in times of drought. Spartia beach, south of the village, is an ideal spot for fishermen and those who prefer isolated beaches. The village of **Korianna** was named after the spice coriander by the ancient Myceneans. The locals, however, believe that it was named in memory of a beautiful girl, Kori Anna, who died young of tuberculosis. The next village, **Klismata**, hold a joint celebration with Korianna for the feast-days of Antimiri and Agios Spiridon on the sand beach of Paliolinos. The traditional food served at the celebration is "riganada", made from dry bread dipped first in water to soften it, and then in olive oil. After adding some fresh tomato, it is topped with oregano and feta cheese. Anyone who has eaten it swears it is delicious! Continuing on the same road, you come to **Kountourata** and **Pessada**, mentioned in 1262 by the same names. In 1800 they were the island's most wealthy villages. Pessada is today a lovely village with some old homes of seafarers. The Church of the Evangelistria, built by the Inglessis family, celebrates its feast-day with a festival on March 25. In a lovely setting a short distance from the village stands the nunnery of the Estavromenos built by the Valsamakis family in 1602. For those who are tired of seeing "NO HUNTING" signs, the Sklavounis farm offers pheasant hunting. Swimmers will limit themselves to Ammos and Goulias beaches.

Dorizata, always a sparsely-populated village, is the birthplace of the prominent politician G. Dorizas, who rescinded the excommunication of the famous Greek author Laskaratos.

Descending through vineyards and olive orchards, we come to **Karavados**, a small village which boasts the excellent sand beach of Agios Thomas. Just before the taverna on the beach, there is a spring of crystal-clear water, surrounded by plane-trees and reeds. The imposing rock known as Geronitsia ("little pieces of old folks") has a blood-curdling history: tradition has it that the ancients did away with their senior citizens by throwing them off this rock.

Surviving in the Church of the Saviour in **Travliata** are the old altar-screen, a 17th-century calendar of holidays and the icon of the Madonna of the Angels by Amvrossios Borinos.

Peratata, a village that dates back to the 15th century, took its name from the word "perasma" (crossing), as it was a crossing for pirates. It is the site of the island's only perfume factory, the Mavro Elato. Above Peratata, on the crest of a pine-blanketed hill, stands the **fortress of Agios Georgios**, which was the centre of the island's religious, social and political life from 1500 until 1759.

The fortress lies at 320 m above sea level, approximately 5 km from the island's present-day capital. It was proba-

The little sand beach of Karavados has a cafeteria and a taverna for weary swimmers!

bly built by Byzantine emperors between 394 and 1185 AD. It served as an observation post for detecting surprise landings of enemy forces or pirates. Its position made it possible to scrutinize the flat country round about; ease of communication with the rest of the island permitted order to be imposed. The fortress provided a place of refuge for the authorities and the people in case of danger. Under the Venetian occupation it served as a headquarters or dwelling-place for the island's rulers (the Orsini and Tocco families, the Turks and the Venetians); the island's gentry also lived there. As population increased inside the fortress (the Borgo), outside it a suburb (Exo Borgo) sprang up. The suburb and the fortress comprised the island's capital until 1759, when it was moved to Argostoli, leaving behind only the bureau of archives, which remained there until 1790. The capital was never very densely populated, because the populace preferred to live in the countryside.

The original dimensions of the fortress are not known, since no pre-1500 plans have been found. In 1504 Kefalonian and Venetian craftsmen built a new enceinte, using the fortification systems which were new at that time. From then on, quite a few additions and improvements were made. The castle as it appears today covers an area of 16,000 square meters and has a circumference of 600 m; polygonal in shape, it is composed of three parts: the outer wall, the inner enceinte and the rocky outcrop in the centre of the enceinte. The winged lion that once stood at the entrance no longer exists. From the interior you can see the crenels and observation posts on the battlements. If you take the uphill path straight in from the entrance, you will come to a small square (Kanoni). On your left are the ruins of the castle's church, dedicated to Agios Georgios. On the cisterns and the outer battlement near the entrance the coats of arms of its noble Venetian inhabitants can still be seen. Farther up, to the right, are the storerooms and prisons. Behind them is what has remained of the bridge that connected the battlements. In case of emergency, the means of escape was a tunnel that led to Koutavos lagoon. There were also private buildings, barracks, hospitals, etc. A tour of the fortress may put you in a bellicose mood; if so,

The fortress of Agios Georgios overlooks the area of Krania and Livathos, up to the shores of Katelios

look out over the fertile fields to the vastness of the sea and a sense of peace will prevail. (Opening hours 8am-8pm weekdays. 8am-2:30pm Sundays. Closed Mondays.)

The inhabitants of the castle, who were known for the fine leather goods they produced, increased in numbers until there were 14,000 of them; they built 15 churches, both Catholic and Orthodox. Still standing on the edge of the present-day picturesque village is the old cathedral of the Evangelistria, with Byzantine icons attributed to Tsankarolos. It holds a festival every year on December 12. Around the hill, in among thick forests of cypresses and pines, the ruins of the Churches of Agios Spiridon and Agii Theodori proudly stand. The Church of Agios Nikolaos was rebuilt in 1504 but burned down in 1726.

Tradition tells us that the hill was haunted before the fortress was built there. The forest of lofty trees and riotous vegetation was inhabited only by fairies. No one dared steal a veil they had and turn them into good, obedient wives. But one day pirates arrived on the island; less superstitious than the locals, they hid in the forest. From it they launched attacks on the surrounding villages, and the forest indeed became a dangerous place. The indignant villagers set fire to the forest, to burn everything they were afraid of, both fairies and pirates. The fire quickly spread, leaving the hill bare. On its peak the chapel of Agios Georgios was built, and it has given its name to the hill.

One of the late Mycenean rock tombs in Mazarakata. The finds it housed are on exhibit in the Archaeological Museum in Argostoli

In **Mazarakata** in 1908 the archaeologist P. Kavadias excavated a late Mycenean burial ground containing a domed masonry tomb and 16 more hollowed out of the rock. The walls of the corridors meet overhead and their floors slant downwards. Between them there are approximately 83 rectangular pits (graves). The burial chamber is circular in shape. The tombs were discovered intact and contained a wealth of grave goods (gold jewelry and pottery), some of which are on exhibit in the Argostoli Museum. Unfortunately, some of the vases have been carried off to museums in Switzerland and London. Between Kokolata and Menegata, in the vicinity of Kangelisses, a pre-Mycenean cemetery was found. Its tombs contained monochrome pottery, a bronze knife and jewelry made of various materials. All the artefacts are now housed in the Archaeological museum.

Argostoli – Lourdata – Sissia – Markopoulo – Skala

To visit this area, which is known as Ikosimia and lies to the west of Mt. Ainos, take the main road in the direction of Poros. The land is mostly flat with olive orchards and vineyards. After **Poriarata**, the road descends for 2 km to the Trapezaki locale by the sea. The fine beach offers a combination of sea amd thick pine woods. In the private Church of the Panagia there is a silver icon of the Virgin that was found by a noblewoman from Pessada. A celebration is held here on the feast-day of the Holy Spirit.

Beginning in the 16th century, the Venetians allowed people from the Peloponnese to relocate in **Moussata** because the area had been deserted after repeated pirate attacks. Grapes for Rombola wine are cultivated here, too. In **Vlahata**'s big Church of Agia Marina, which managed to survive the earthquakes, a saint's day celebration featuring folk dancing is held every July 17. You now leave the main road again and head for the large seaside village of **Lourdata**. In the village square stands a hugh plane-tree; springs have flowed out from among its roots for the past 200 years. Local women once did their laundry in the stone troughs here. A footpath above the square leads to the Byzantine Church of Agia Paraskevi. The road ends up at the bow-shaped sand beach of

The Chapel of the Panagia in Trapezaki

The superb sand beach in Trapezaki, one of the island's most-frequented

The plane-tree in Lourdata square

Lourdas, with its small tavernas. It attracts most of the area's holiday-makers. Conditions in Lourdata are such that tropical plants, including bananas, can be grown. Water coming down from Mt. Ainos is used for irrigation, the area is sheltered from chilling winds, and the reflection of the sun's rays off the sides of Mt. Ainos create relatively high temperatures. The area's garden produce is some of the best on the island.

Continue on the main road through **Simotata**, where a delicious cheese known as prentza is produced. A turnoff from the main road leads to the old monastery of Sissia (13th century). It is said to have been founded by and named after St. Francis of Assisi, who followed the Crusaders to Syria and Egypt; on the return journey in 1218, heavy seas forced his ship to land in Kefalonia. The monastery later became the brunt of pirate attacks, whereupon the monks of the order of St. Francis abandoned it. It turned Orthodox in the 16th century, and was dedicated to the Dormition of the Virgin of Sissia. It was completely demolished in the 1953 earthquakes, and today it stands in ruins just below the new monastery. The custom of carrying the 13th-century icon of the Panagia (which St. Francis dedicated to the monastery) to the castle every year on the feast-day of St. Thomas and bringing it back two weeks later was initiated in 1676.

Back on the main road, you come to

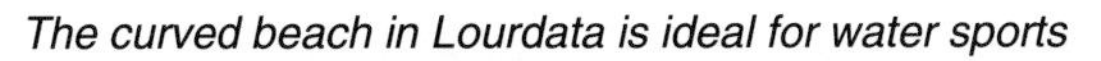

The curved beach in Lourdata is ideal for water sports

The new monastery of the Dormition of the Virgin of Sissia in Simotata

Brightly-painted outer walls and tidy flower gardens create a feeling of familiarity

the seaside area of Eleios, said to owe its name to the mythical hero Eleios, son of the king of Helida and ally of Cephalus. The scene here consists of level ground with olive-trees and vineyards, and offers a marvellous view of the sea. The first village you will encounter is **Platies**, where there are a few rooms to rent. One kilometer further on, you will reach an intersection. The road on the right leads to **Hionata**; from there a narrower road makes the round of this area and then intersects with the road to Skala. Not to be missed in this part of the island is the Monastery of Agios Dionissios, rebuilt in 1963 as it was before the earthquakes. It is a subsidiary of the Monastery of Agios Dionissios in Zakinthos, where the left hand of St. Dionissios is kept. Its festival day is November 17. The next villages are **Valeriano** and **Thiramonas**. On a hill stands the lovely Church of Ai-Giannis. An unpaved but passable road on the right begins at the Church of Agios Dimitrios and winds up below a cliff in Skali,

The seaside village of Kato Katelios

whose nearby beaches offer beauty and isolation. Two km further down the road you encounter **Mavrata**, well-known for the precious finds from a sealed domed tomb of some person of note which was excavated nearby. The roof of the tomb has now caved in.

Another kilometer further on, the main road descends to the seaside village of **Kato Katelios**, on the edge of the Katelios basin. This village is particularly well-liked by tourists for its long stretch of crenellated coast, not to mention the tavernas serving fresh fish and local wine. You can, of course, catch your own fish in Katelios Bay and one of the congenial

Yet another of Kefalonia's many long beaches, in Katelios

The string of beaches at Ratzakli, one of the favourite nesting-places of the very ancient Loggerhead Turtle (Caretta caretta). Females swim for thousands of miles about every three years to return to the beach where they were hatched and lay their eggs in the hot sand

taverna-keepers will be happy to cook it for you.

Mounda Bay in **Ratzakli** has two lovely beaches in a row. The first is Kaminia ("kilns"), which took its name from the kilns where roof-tiles used to be made from a type of clay found in the area. The second is Potamakia, with shallow water and golden sands, one of the places the endangered Loggerhead Turtle (Caretta caretta) lays its eggs. Turtles may be found on any of the beaches on the south side of Kefalonia. You are requested not to disturb their nests, which are often marked.

Skala is a seaside resort village built after the earthquakes. It was built at a lower elevation than the original village,

The Loggerhead Turtle can reach a length of about 1.2 m and a weight of 100 kilograms

The seaside resort of Skala has all the modern tourist facilities

Skala beach is justified in being the main pole of attraction for visitors to the area

which was up on the hillside. The area is known as Mi Ambeli, from its many vineyards (vineyard=ambeli). The pine grove and the vast golden sand beach, ideal for water sports, are reason enough to visit Skala, as many tourists do each year. A carefree atmosphere, bars, Greek nightclubs, appealing tavernas and a vibrant nightlife are some of the resort's other attractions.

In 1957 excavations began on the villa of a wealthy Roman, which housed hot springs. It was discovered accidentally by the owner of the land in 1944, but its existence was mentioned as far back as 1822 by the archaeologist Goodisson. Its main interest lies in its well-preserved mosaics and 3rd-century inscriptions. In the villa's first room there is a mosaic depicting a naked youth, Envy. He is clutching his throat with his hands while four wild beasts attack him. Obviously this is Envy being choked by his malice, suffering as he watches some happy person. In the second room the mosaic shows the sacrifice of a bull, a ram and a boar, reminiscent of Roman suovetaurilia, commonplace in the area of Greece and possibly a foretaste of the new religion. It was made by the artisan Krateros and his son. In Byzantine times, the Church of Agios Athanassios was built over the villa's third room, and in the fourth room there is a mosaic floor with geometrical designs.

Taking the narrow dirt road that runs along the seashore from Skala to Poros,

Smaller, isolated sand beaches near Skala

you will reach the Sakkos taverna in about one km. From there you can ask someone to guide you to Sakkos cave, which is believed to have been used in prehistoric times, as stone-age implements have come to light in the area. Another kilometer further on stands the chapel of Agios Georgios. Still to be seen are the ruins of an ancient temple of Apollo made of porous stone. It was built in the 6th century BC, and later provided some of the building materials for the chapel. The Archaeological Museum in Argostoli has an extremely ancient Doric column capital which later served as a pedestal for the chapel's altar.

On the way back you can take the road to **Markopoulo**, a village built on a prominence like a natural balcony, commanding a panoramic view. The Church of the Panagia of Langouvarda burned in 1945 and fell in the earthquakes in 1953. At the new church built on the same site, a unique religious phenomenon occurs every year at the festival of the Dormition of the Virgin on August 15. The most honoured guests at the festival are the small non-poisonous snakes which have a black mark like a cross on their heads and tongues. On the night of August 6, they creep in droves to gather on the church's courtyard wall, bell-tower and the silver icon of the Panagia Fidou (Virgin of the Snakes). Worshippers are photographed with the snakes, and not only are they unafraid of this usually alarming reptile, but in fact they consider it holy. After the festival the snakes withdraw quietly, only to return at the same time the following year.

The church was formerly located in another part of the island and was used as a nunnery. During a pirate raid, the nuns, terrified at the thought of the outrages usually committed by pirates, begged the Virgin to turn them into snakes. Tradition has it that when the pirates entered the nunnery all they found were snakes. The locals believe

The famous Monastery of the Panagia of Langouvarda in Markopoulo

the emergence of the snakes to be an indication of good luck. That won't seem so strange to you when you learn that during the German occupation and in the years of the island's great earthquakes the sacred snakes failed to make their customary visits to the village!

The next village you will come to is **Kolaitis**, at 500 m above sea level. Higher up lies the hamlet of **Arginia**, with the monastery of Zoodohos Pigi. In **Atsoupades** be sure to taste some of the pure honey produced there. The village may have taken its name from Atsipada in Crete, some of whose families fled to Kefalonia to escape the Turks. The name is Byzantine and means dark-complexioned person.

The small mountain hamlet of Arginia

Argostoli – Tzanata – Poros – Ainos

You will pass Markopoulo once more. The road leads up to the mountain village of **Kremidi**, with a view of the valley. In the Church of Panagia Gravaliotissa in **Pastra**, the Madonna lilies bloom on the 15th of August every year.

On the hill beyond Pastra lay the ancient city of **Pronnoi**; according to the ancient historian Polybius, it was difficult to conquer. All that remains today in the imposing triangular hulk of the castle of Paleokastro is the ruins of the walls of the acropolis. It is popularly known as Kastro tis Sirias or Kastro tis Orias.

Thucydides mentions Cyclopean walls from prehistoric times here. The city's fortifications, the fortresses in nearby areas and archaeological evidence all confirm the existence of a rather powerful city. In Skala there was an ancient sandstone quarry, and a section of Mt. Ainos belonged to the inhabitants of Pronnoi. It was also the first city to ally itself with Athens in the Second Athenian Confederacy. It was in Skala that the Pronnians had their seat under the Macedonians. In the foothills of Paleokastro, above the road we are travelling on, a necropolis from the Classical and early Christian eras was discovered.

After Pastra, a turnoff to the right takes us off the main road onto a passable dirt road which leads to **Alimatas** and **Fanies**. Another unpaved road to the left brings us to the ruins of the old Church of Panagia Theofanitria dating from the 15th century. Its only remaining fresco is a fine one of the burning bush. In the village of **Kotrokoi** stands the old church of Profitis Ilias.

The shady dirt road now leads up through dense vegetation to **Asprogerakas**. Before coming out on the asphalt paved road to Poros, we encounter the ruined monastery of Agios Nikolaos at the Halikiopoulou locale. It belongs to the monastery of Agios Gerassimos; in 1598 the nuns of Atros, pursued by the Turks, took refuge here.

The Church of the Panagia Gravaliotissa in Pastra

The Church of Agios Nikolaos in Asprogerakas

The village of Xenopoulo, drenched in greenery

Those who want to get to Poros quickly should take the road through **Agia Irini** or **Arakli**, which took its name from the mythical hero Heracles. On an unpaved road to the left is the 14th-century "Palace of the Count" (Palati tou Konte). Ask someone living nearby to let you in to see it.

Poros can also be reached on the **Agios Georgios** turnoff; after a dismal 6-km. drive through burned forest we come to the mountain village of **Kapandriti** with quaint little coffee-shops. At a distance of one km. on an unpaved road lies **Xenopoulo**, rebuilt not far from its original site. Its hospitable inhabitants will show you the old chapel of the Panagia, in the vicinity of Trahonia. After the villages of **Andriolata** and **Kambitsata**, in the eastern foothills of Mt. Ainos, the road follows a purling brook lined with plane-trees as far as **Tzanata**. You can taste local specialties in the taverna in the shade of a huge plane-tree.

I must mention here that, in their efforts to locate Homeric Ithaca, certain archaeologists came to believe that Odysseus' island was Kefalonia and not Ithaki. The excavations carried out at the Brouzi locale in Tzanata in June, 1991 by the Patras Director of Antiquities, L. Kolonas, caused quite a stir in Kefalonia and Ithaki. Artefacts found there are highly significant and unique in the Greek area: an impressive domed tomb of a distinguished person dating from 1400-1050 BC, various desecrated tombs, gold jewelry and seals. Undoubtedly the area has all the conditions that would indicate the presence of a powerful Mycenean centre (thick vegetation, water, proximity to the Mt. Ainos fir-forest, sheltered harbour near mainland Greece) and experts have high hopes of being able to pinpoint the

The fine vaulted tomb of a prominent person from 1400-1050 BC, in the Brouzi locale in Tzanata

The "Poros Defile", a miniature version of the Tempi valley

site of Odysseus' city. Investigations are continuing at the site: anyone who wants to draw his own conclusions has only to ask the Chairman of the Commune for a guided tour.

Our route continues through green hills and gorges, and winds up in Poros, in the middle of the "Poros Defile", a miniature version of the Tempi Valley. This wild, majestic terrain is associated with a strange myth, which tells us that the indentations in the rocks are Heracles' supernaturally gigantic footprints; the arrogant hero did not deign to take the normal road to reach his destination.

The seaside town of **Poros** is one of the island's two main harbours. It has been inhabited since Classical times. It was renamed Nea Malta when it was settled by Maltesians whom Napier brought here out of fear that the area would be deserted. The model farming community he intended to create never went into operation.

This constantly developing tourist area offers a combination of mountains and sea. It boasts hotels, rooms to rent and souvenir shops. On the left side of town next to the sea are modern restaurants and traditional small tavernas. On

Poros' seaside road is lined with modern restaurants and traditional tavernas serving local specialties

the beach, site of the harbour of ancient Pronnoi, you can use the volleyball, tennis and basketball courts and of course engage in water sports. You will be surprised at how clean a beach next to a port can be! Another surprise awaits fishing enthusiasts, as Poros is a rich fishing grounds, with many different fish species.

Several cultural events take place each summer. The Poros Philharmonic participates in many of them.

A dirt road, ideal for testing the capabilities of your four-wheel-drive vehicle, runs up the Atros massif. On its peak, at

Diaphanous blue-green waters off Poros beach, ideal for swimming and fishing

A panoramic view of the seaside town of Poros, as seen from the historic Monastery of the Theotokos of Atros

Much-frequented Poros beach teems with life all summer long

535 m. above sea level, stands the island's oldest monastery, the historic **Monastery of the Theotokos of Atros**. The first reference to this monastery is contained in a report of the Latin Archbishopric of Cephallenia in 1248. Don't let the steep climb deprive you of the unique view of Poros, the tranquillity and if possible the sunrise.

Back in Tzanata, take the road up to the mountainous Pirgi region, the closest to Mt. Ainos. The villages here offer a striking contrast to the lusher villages in the valley of Pronnoi and Poros; they are, however, famous for their animal products. By following the brook that waters the fields in the valley, you come to **Agios Nikolaos**. On the outskirts of the village, a short distance from the road at 300 m. above sea level, lies the well-known Lake **Avithos** or **Megali Akoli**; its name denotes the islanders' conviction that it is bottomless. The lake's abundant water irrigates the valley. On the other side of the mountain at the same elevation is Lake Mikri Akoli, now dry, which is believed to have been connected to Megali Akoli at one time. In **Harakti** you will see the ruins of an ancient fortress and of the old Church of the Archangels. Near the Church of Agios Nikolaos in Koutoupakia, the villagers, fearful of

The village of Agios Nikolaos

Nowadays no one still believes that the small lake of Avithos or Megali Akoli is really bottomless

View of the village of Harakti

Quaint islanders will welcome you and show you around their villages

Turkish robbers, hid their gold in their cisterns; it has never been found.

After new **Digaleto** (the original village was located higher up), we come to **Tsakarissiano**, whose new houses lie scattered over the hill. The church-bells of the old village, destroyed by the Turks, are buried somewhere near the country chapel of Agios Nikolaos, on the side where the sun rises. The area most important sight to see is the ruined Sordatos Castle, which served as a watch-tower for the ancient city of Pronnoi.

In the village of Tsakarissiano stand the ruins of one of the watch-towers of ancient Pronnoi

Argostoli – Monastery of Agios Gerassimos – Mt. Ainos – Sami – Karavomilos

This itinerary takes us through the Omala valley which extends as far as the foothills of Mt. Ainos. The first village we come to it **Mitikata**. The narrow concrete-paved road runs between courtyards overflowing with Bougainvillaeas up to the ruins of the Church of Agios Nikolaos. It may be worth your while to make a quick detour from the main road to see the Church of the Panagia in **Demoutsantata**. Another strange event occurs here every year on August 23, the Church's festival day, when a lily which is dried up for the rest of the year blooms before the icon of the Virgin. Coming into **Troianata**, we encounter the Church of Agia Paraskevi, whose feast-day is celebrated on July 26, and that of Agios Dimitrios, built in 1840, which managed to survive the earthquakes unscathed.

View of Omala valley

Descending to the valley, we can see the island's largest and most majestic monastery, the **Monastery of Agios Gerassimos**, the island's patron saint. It draws many tourists to the island every year. At its entrance stands a splendid bell-tower built in the architectural style peculiar to the Ionian islands. The saint's relics are kept here in a silver reliquary; they are exhibited in a shrine in the monastery's smaller church. A small hole in its floor leads 4-5 meters down to an underground chamber, which is joined to another, even smaller chamber on the same level, where the saint lived as a hermit. His memory is celebrated in two great festivals, one on August 16, the date of his death (the real date was August 15, but because this coincides with the Dormition of the Virgin, it has been set a day later.) and the other on October 20 (the date his relics were removed from his tomb). During both festivals, the saint's mortal remains are carried in an upright position in a procession for 500 meters. The procession starts out from the church and proceeds down a

An icon of Agios Gerassimos from the Tipaldon-Iakovaton Museum in Lixouri

Carrying the relics of Agios Gerassimos in a procession in Omala before the earthquake (1950)

Carrying the relics of Agios Gerassimos in a procession on the feast-day of Agios Thomas (1993)

wide road lined with poplars as far as a spreading plane-tree where there is a well said to have been dug by the saint himself. A hostel with a capacity of 20 accommodates a few of the thousands of visitors to these festivals.

Agios Gerassimos was born Gerassimos Notaras in 1507 in Trikala, Korinthia; he was the scion of a wealthy family of refugees from Constantinople. From an early age he shown an inclination to live a monastic life: when still in his youth he left his family to study at the School of Zakinthos. In 1537 he went to Jerusalem. He stayed there for 12 years, was ordained a monk and returned to Greece. He journeyed first to Crete and then to Zakinthos, where he lived for four years

The present-day monastery bears no resemblance to the one pictured in this 1866 engraving (Korgialenio Museum). *It has been expanded due to the dozens of visitors who are drawn to it each year by the Saint's reputed miracles*

The superb bell-tower at the entrance to the monastery

in a cave near Agios Georgios Gremnon. In 1554 he came to Kefalonia and lived for another 6 years near the Spilia locale, in a cave he had visited on his first trip to the island. In 1560 he went to the Omala valley, where there was an abandoned chapel dedicated to the Virgin. There he established a nunnery which he named New Jerusalem. At the same time he taught the children of the nearby villages their lessons.

It is said that when he planted plane-trees in the nunnery he was asked how he expected water-loving trees to grow on such dry ground. He replied that it was God's job to look after them. He died on August 15, 1579. After two years, during which repeated miracles took place, his body was disinterred and found to be intact. It was disinterred again in another 8 months and was still in perfect condition. The ecclesiastical authorities of Kefalonia then petitioned the Patriarch of Constantinople, who declared Gerassimos Notaras a saint. Many miracles are attributed to Agios Gerassimos: most of them have to do with exorcisms of demons.

The villages around the nunnery are the major producers of a wine of excellent quality, Rombola, known throughout the world. The headquarters of the Rombola co-operative is in **Valsamata**. In **Frangata**, a well-laid-out village rebuilt after the earthquakes with British help in a new location, the Rombola wine festival is held on the first Saturday after Agios Gerassimos' feast-day every August.

The folklorist V. Karoussos, in the Argostoli newspaper "Anamorfossis", tells the strange story of an event said to have taken place in one of the Omala villages; it is rather reminiscent of a tale from Transylvania. A certain Loretzatos was believed to be a vampire, and so he was buried with a coin and a knife. Thorns were placed all around him. The coin was probably intended to be his fare to Hades. His grave was dug near water, so the dead man wouldn't get thirsty. A hole was dug and wheat was placed in it; he would be able to cut the wheat with his knife and eat it. The thorns were to keep him in his grave!

After coming out on the main road, turn right towards **Agios Eleftherios**. From here a passable but unpaved road takes you up for one kilometre to the Mt.

Splendid views of the island from the peak of its tallest mountain, Ainos

The famous Cephalonian Fir is a distinctive species of fir-tree with whitish branches and sharp needles

Ainos tourist pavilion, at an elevation of 1,300 m. The road was built at the time of Napier, who took care to preserve the forest. From here the going is on foot up to the highest peak, Megas Soros (1,628 m.). The view is stupendous, with Zakinthos out in the distance, Ithaki to the east and beyond it Lefkada. On a clear day, even the peaks of Kerkira (Corfu) are visible! This hike is a must for every nature-lover. In the two upper zones of vegetation, the predominant tree is the indigenous Cephalonian Fir (Abies cephalonica).

This tree consists of an erect trunk of a burnt-looking colour and whitish branches that fork out from the trunk near the base of the tree, giving it a bushy appearance. The branches do not bend downward, as in most firs, but upward. Its needles are thicker at the base, tapering down to sharp points. When the cones ripen, they shed their scales, leaving only bare spindles. Because of the dark green blanket of firs that covered Mt. Ainos, Venetian sailors named it Monte Nero (Black Mountain).

Kefalonia owes its pre-eminence in prehistoric times to the lumber trade. The columns in the palace in Knossos were made of Cephalonian fir. Later, the island's forest supplied shipyards in Corfu and Italy with lumber. This harvesting, together with repeated fires, greatly reduced its size. The great fire of 1590 burned three quarters of the forest. Nevertheless, as late as 1793, according to the historian Lomverdos, the forest still covered the greater part of both sides of the mountain, an area 13 km wide and 5 km long. Two more fires occurred in 1730 and 1760. But the worst of all, in 1797, caused incalculable damage. It started when the watchman let farmers plant in the extremely fertile soil next to the forest; up to that time it had been forbidden to plant there. The fire they set to clear off the land spread quickly, the wind was against them, and there was no rain. It is said that for the duration of the fire (three months!) the nights in the town of Argostoli were as light as the days. The destruction of the forest brought about a change in the island's climate (hotter summers, colder winters). In 1962 this invaluable forest was declared a National Park. Mt. Ainos has snow from the beginning of December to the end of March, but there is no question of skiing!

Ruins of the temple of Aenesian Zeus, from which smoke-signals were sent to all the other temples of Zeus when it was time for a sacrifice to begin

Below Megas Soros stand the ruins of the sanctuary of Aenesian Zeus, mentioned by Hesiod. Worship of the god dates from the end of the 8th century BC. Still visible are the bones of animals which were sacrificed there.

The sanctuary has associations with the myth of the Harpies, those dirty, evil, winged monsters with beautiful long hair. They caused unimaginable distress to the blind soothsayer Phineas, since every time he got ready to eat, they flew in and took away his food. The scraps that were left were so dirty that it was impossible no human being could possibly eat them. This situation continued until the Argonauts reached the land of Pontus and asked for the soothsayer's help, so that they could resume their journey to Colchis. In return he asked them to kill the Harpies. The lot fell to the sons

Recently the amazing wild horses in the Mt. Ainos National Park have fallen victim to human brutality!

The natural balcony formed when the roof of Drongarati cave fell in

of Boreus. The first Harpy was quickly overcome and fell into a river in the Peloponnese, known as Harpyis. The second flew towards the sacred mountains of the Echinadae (the Ionian islands), and so the Argonauts asked for help from Aenesian Zeus. Exhausted, the Harpy fell near the islets known as Strofades.

Still living on Mt. Ainos are the twelve remaining wild horses of Kefalonia. They are believed to be descended from a very rare ancient breed of horses. But don't set your hopes on seeing them, because these shy animals will hide as soon as they hear or smell your presence.

The main road goes on to Sami, in an area known for its picturesque beaches and numerous geological phenomena such as caves and underground lakes. The most impressive cave is **Drongarati**, which experts have estimated to be about 150 million years old. The island-

On this 100-square-meter platform famous musicians have given concerts in the past

The small hamlet of Zervata in the green valley of Sami

ers have known about the cave for over a hundred years, but it was only in 1963 that it was developed to accommodate visitors. It was damaged in the earthquakes and a section of its roof has caved in. A downhill corridor leads to a natural balcony overlooking a chamber with about 100 square meters of floor space. It houses rare stalactites and stalagmites, and its acoustics are excellent. A special platform was set up at the far end of the cave, making it possible to hold concerts here; at one time up to 500 people would flock to the cave to hear well-known musicians!

Before you come to Sami, a turnoff to the right leads to **Haliotata**, a village that escaped devastation in the earthquakes. A few blackened trees are a reminder of the need to prevent forest fires. In **Katapodata**, don't be fooled by the restored exterior of the Church of Agios Spiridon; the interior remains as it was before the quakes. In **Grizata** and **Zervata** you will find honey and wine of excellent quality. After **Koulourata**, the road runs along beside a stream lined with plane-trees, towards Poros. You can now return to the main road between Argostoli and Sami.

Sami or **Gialos** is the island's second largest port. The modern town, built after the 1953 earthquakes at the foot of the hills of Agii Fanentes and Kastro with assistance from the British, has lost none of the importance it had in ancient times.

As in all the island's seaside towns, people in Sami gather at nightfall in the establishments on the seaside promenade to have some fun

The 18th-century chapel of Agios Nikolaos, on Agii Fanentes Hill, where the acropolis of ancient Cyatis once stood

Its hotels, restaurants, campsites and archaeological and geological points of interest attract a large share of the island's tourists.

Sami was one of the island's four ancient cities. It occupied an important geographic position. In the Homeric epics, Samos or Same (quite possibly a reference to the whole island) is mentioned as having participated in the Trojan War. Another passage states that 24 of the Penelope's 108 suitors were from Same. As a self-governing city-state, Same had its own coins; they and other artefacts from the excavations of the acropoleis testify to the town's wealth as well as to the density of its population.

Behind the town rise the two hills on which the ancient city was built. One of them, Agii Fanentes, took its name from the three saints buried here. Lord Byron stayed for a night in the hostel near the church here. At the foot of this hill, in a fenced-in area, stands a well-preserved building from the Roman era. The locals call it Rakospito (a corruption of Drakospito); it most likely housed Roman baths (hot springs). Near it a superb mosaic was discovered in 1956, and two years later an extraordinarily fine bronze head

The bronze head of a Roman from the 3rd century AD (Archaeological Museum, Argostoli)

Romantic boat-rides and fishing at sunset in Sami (G. Papadatos collection)

The unpretentious bells of the Agrilion Monastery, hanging on one of its many olive-trees

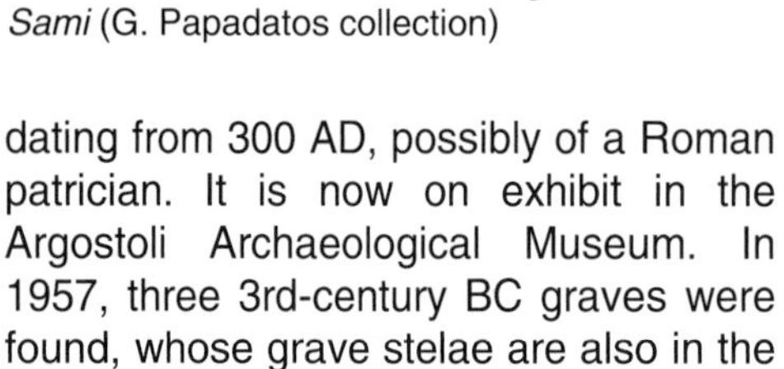

dating from 300 AD, possibly of a Roman patrician. It is now on exhibit in the Argostoli Archaeological Museum. In 1957, three 3rd-century BC graves were found, whose grave stelae are also in the Archaeological Museum in Argostoli.

A narrower road on the right leads to the acropoleis, 7 km further up. On the pine-clad hill of Agii Fanentes stands the acropolis of Cyatis, and on the rocky hill of Kastro is the acropolis of Megisto Toxo. Still standing are the two gates and the rectangular stone blocks that formed their Mycenean walls. The gate to the Kastro acropolis is very similar to the one in Mycenae. The Church of Agios Nikolaos with important 18th-century frescos now stands on the site of the acropolis of Cyatis.

East of Sami, the road forks. Continue straight on for the superb beach of Antissamos, with milky-white shingles and blue-green waters enclosed by green hills. The uphill unpaved but passable

Blue-green waters and lush vegetation on the vast beach of Antissamos – one of the island's loveliest

road on the right leads to the Monastery of Theotokos Agrilion, built on the top of the hill at an elevation of 180 m in the midst of wild olive-trees. Most of it has been repaired since the earthquakes of 1953. That was when a stone slab dating from 1721 with religious subjects in relief was discovered; you can see it next to the throne. In the monastery's inner courtyard a stone prie-dieu stands on the spot where the ascetic Cosmas the Aetolian once taught. A procession and festival are held in his honour every year on August 24.

Agios Cosmas was born in 1714 in Aetolia. When he had completed his studies in a school on Holy Mt. Athos, he began his work as a missionary. This fiery preacher of humble sentiments and artless appearance visited Kefalonia in June 1777. He preached in Assos, Komitata, Plagia Erissou, the Thematon Monastery and the Agrilion Monastery.

At the Agii Theodori locale there are ruins of Mycenean houses, and one kilometre outside Same is the Fitidi cave, which was used in Palaeolithic times.

On the road from Sami to Agia Efimia you will come to the village of **Poulata**. Throughout this area there are small caves, undeveloped for tourism, which are nevertheless important; most enclose small lakes. Don't try to find them on your own, because you will most likely get lost on the primitive dirt roads. Again, ask for help from the locals. To the south-east of Poulata is the cave of Agalaki, whose entrance is a vertical shaft 30 m deep. Its roof has caved in, forming a pile of rubble 10 m in height. Its two passageways lead to pools 10 m deep whose water reflects the stalactites hanging from the ceiling. To the north is another pit-cave, Agii Theodori, which reaches a depth of 55 m. The galleries in this cave also lead to pools. Further to the west is the Agia Eleoussa pit-cave, hidden in thick vegetation. Its depth is 65 m. Another pit-cave with a depth of 40 m is Hiridoni, with an inclined floor that gradually becomes submerged and a gallery filled with water.

Karavomilos (old Vlahata), 2 km after Sami, is another one of the villages that was rebuilt after the earthquakes. On the village fringe, behind the Church of Agios Ioannis, lies the lake of Karavomilos. Salt-water from Melissani cave gushes up from the lake bottom; it then empties into Sami Bay through the underground conduits known as the Katavothres. At the tourist pavilion you can enjoy an iced coffee while watching the ducks on the lake. In this general area there are several tavernas and rooms to rent.

Near Karavomilos is another pit-cave, Zervati, with a depth of 18 m and pools of fresh water. Here also is island's most impressive lake and cave, **Melissani** (Blue Cave). Leave your car on the parking lot and go down into the entrance to

The magnificent Church of Agios Pandeleimon in Poulata

Karavomilos Lake, into which water from Lake Melissani empties

In front of picturesque Karavomilos Lake, the Church of Agios Ioannis, together with its bell-tower, complete a beautiful picture

the cave. Even in summer the air will feel cool and damp. Boats are waiting at the shore to take you around the lake. Each boatman will use his rudimentary English, French and Italian to compare the stalactites to various animals in a humorous way.

The cave is 100 m long; one-third of its space is taken up by the lake, which has a depth is 36 m. It was officially discovered by Austrian divers and was first opened to visitors in 1963. The islanders were aware of its existence much earlier: a shepherdess had fallen into the lake while trying to find a lost sheep. The cave's stalactites are over 20,000 years old. The lake's water empties into the lake in Karavomilos.

After the 1953 earthquakes the ceiling of the cave fell in, creating what may be one of the most impressive sights you have ever seen. In July and August, between 10:30 am and 1:00 pm, the rays of the sun enter and transform the colour of the water; the various shades of blue are then reflected onto the walls of the cave. The cave is also of archaeological interest: in 1951, Petrohilos found an ancient lantern on the island at the entrance to the second chamber. On the same site in 1963, excavations led by Marinatos revealed a clay figurine of the god Pan, a disc bearing a representation of Pan surrounded by dancing nymphs, and a rectangular fragment with the figure of a woman in relief (she may be the nymph Melissanthe, whose name has been corrupted to Melissani). The finds are exhibited in the Archaeological Museum in Argostoli.

The whole place has an aura of mystery about it. Perhaps it is the troubled soul of the nymph who loved Pan, and drowned in the lake when he rejected her.

I believe a boat-ride on the mysterious blue-green waters of Melissani Lake to be a unique experience. Archaeological finds from there are now on exhibit in the Archaeological Museum

The lovely Church of Agios Ioannis Hrissostomos commands a view from the hill above Kourouklata village

Scenes from the procession held on August 15

The village of Zola above Agia Kiriaki Bay

Argostoli – Mirtos – Agia Efimia

Follow the seaside road in the direction of Assos. This road runs through the Thinea region, where the well-known wine of Thinea is produced. The villages here keep up their old traditions, including folk dancing, so don't miss a chance to be present at one of their saint's-day festivals.

You pass through **Davgata**, with its venerable gnarled olive-trees, and **Farsa**, where the facades of the pre-earthquake village stand on the hill. "Telonia", a type of gremlin or leprechaun, is also the name given by the island's sailors to the constellation of Gemini. In antiquity, it was believed that Zeus marvelled at the brotherly love of the twins Castor and Pollux and transformed them into stars to guide ships.

Overlooking the lovely village of **Kourouklata** is the Church of Agios Ioannis Hrissostomos. In **Kontogourata** you can see the Church of the Saviour; not to be missed is the traditional festival on the beach on August 6. A turnoff to the right leads to **Kardakata**. Continuing on the main road to Lixouri, you reach the village of **Zola**, which offers a few rooms to rent. You then head down to the Bay of Agia Kiriaki, with its large beach, a fine place to swim and fish. You need not go up to the village for a meal, as there are tavernas on the beach.

Returning to the main road, you will pass through **Riza**, **Petrikata** and **Nifi**, before coming to **Angonas**. Angonas is also accessible on the unpaved road linking it to Zola. In the village's main square, there are wall-paintings by the folk artist G. Livadas a.k.a. "Razos". Above the square the road leads to the Church of the Panagia.

After another 8 km on the seaside road, you come to **Divarata** or **Siniori** (named after a nobleman who lived in the

Blue-green water and white sand in Agia Kiriaki Bay

area). The author T. Potamianos was born and buried in this village. The Church of Ipapanti is worth seeing.

On the left, a road runs downhill for 4 km to a paradise on earth, the unique beach of Mirtos. It is justifiably considered to be one of the most beautiful beaches in Greece. At the foot of a steep cliff lies the white ribbon of sand, with tiny white pebbles mixed in, and the serene diaphanous water which is quite deep. On our left as we face the sea is a small cave with two entrances, one landward and the other seaward. A small bar on the beach stays open until the small hours. Groups of people light fires here and there on the beach.

The area we are now entering is known as Pilaros (two gates). Twelve of the villages here are built on the slopes of Mt. Agia Dinati, and another twelve on the slopes of Mt. Kalonoros. Before the earthquakes, Pilaros had 24 villages, as many as there are hours in the day, and the whole island had 365, as many as

A fresco by the folk artist G. Livadas in Angonas. The inscription tells about the joy of youth

The ancient philosopher Aristotle contemplated how Kefalonia's sheep got water to drink

Flowers and ruins in Karoussata

there are days in the year. The villagers here still keep up their local traditions. Traditional music and dancing are performed at the local celebrations on Easter and during Carnival season.

On the mountain of Agia Dinati there is believed to have been a temple of Hera. Weird things happen to the sheep, goats and rabbits that graze on its slopes. Because the soil contains mica, many of the animals' teeth look like they are gold- or silver-plated! And while we're on the subject of animals, shepherds here assure us that they don't water their herds between the months of October and May! Aristotle mentions that the animals get the moisture they need by turning their heads into the wind and breathing in moist air from the sea. Housewives in these villages roast meat in an unusual type of cooking utensil, the tsepera, made of clay and goat-hair.

After Divarata you will pass through the lovely gardens of **Karoussata**. The road continues on to the village of **Logarata**, where a few rooms may be found to rent. After another two km. you encounter **Raftopoulata** and **Ferentinata**, birthplace of the champion of democracy M. Antipas. At the entrance to the village you are welcomed by the splendid Church of the Saviour and its once imposing, now fallen, bell-tower. The

The bell-tower of the Church of the Saviour in Ferentinata

church holds its saint's-day celebrations on August 6. It was at just such a celebration many years ago that certain Kefalonians who had made their fortunes abroad decided to take up a collection to build a bell-tower for their church. Before a day had passed, they had collected four large tins of gold coins. Using Russian plans and porous stone from Malta, master builders from Metsovo (who also made the carved wooden altar-screen inside the church) erected a Gothic bell-tower 33 m high! On the way down to the plain, at the Krini locale there are wells and running water, where the locals bring their animals to drink and where in former times they washed wool to make mattresses for newly-weds. The region is beautiful to see in spring. The next village you come to is **Antipata Pilarou**.

In **Dendrinata** don't miss the carved wooden altar-screen in the Church of

Sometimes no words can describe the beauty of nature, as on the beach of Mirtos

Boats in the harbour of Agia Efimia

Agios Konstantinos, and in Hamolakos the chapel of Agios Grigorios, whose altar-screen was made by the father and brother of M. Antipas, both carpenters by trade, with help from Antipas himself.

From **Xeropotamos** you head down to the seaside town of **Agia Efimia**. Before the 1953 earthquakes it was one of the island's more important centres of trade, with stately homes, like the mansion still standing on the right-hand edge of town. Agia Efimia was rebuilt with assistance from the French, and today it is a picturesque provincial town with a small harbour which accommodates yachts and ferry-boats. Its excellent street-plan was laid out in 1878 and it boasts many tourist amenities including hotels and restaurants. Its inhabitants fish for a living or work in the tourist industry. In Lithovati harbour and on the seaside road to Sami there are dozens of small beaches with pebbles and stratified rocks. The largest and most frequented is that of Agia Paraskevi.

The area owes its name to the small white Church of Agia Efimia near the harbour. It celebrates its saint's-day on July 11, with a procession and festival, where the local dance ensemble performs traditional dances. The important altar-screen from the Church of Agios Nikolaos is housed in the Byzantine Museum in Athens. In Arheotiton Street opposite the Moustakis Hotel, a mosaic floor was discovered which had either been part of a Roman villa or had been the original floor in the Church of Agia Efimia. On May Day there is a flower and book show followed by festivities on the beach.

Take the road to the left of the Church of Agios Nikolaos up to **Drakopoulata**, a lovely village left untouched by the earthquakes. In a forest of Laurel trees known as Dafnias stands the Monastery of Panagia to Skalopati.

Before you reach Vassilopoulata,

The local dance troupe performs traditional dances (Moustakis collection)

The lovely little beach of Agia Paraskevi between Agia Efimia and Karavomilos

Visitors to Agia Efimia usually prefer to swim at the small beach in front of the harbour

there is an unpaved road that leads up to an elevation of 500 m above sea level (a 4-wheel-drive vehicle would be desirable here). To your left is Falaris Hill, which took its name from the tyrant Phalares. On its crest is the **Monastery of Theotokos Thematon**, commanding a marvellous view out toward Ithaki. The monastery dates from 1100 AD; in 1500 it had about 42 monks. It fell in the earthquakes in 1953 and was rebuilt in 1970. On the Tuesday after Easter, the monastery holds a mass and a festival. In front of it stands a forest of lofty Kerm-Oaks with concrete benches suitable for picnics. The absolute silence is interrupted only by the chirping of birds and tinkling of sheep-bells.

When you leave Agia Efimia, take the road that runs parallel to the foothills of Megiavouno towards Potamianata. After about a kilometre, there is a fenced-in area about 50 m to the right of the road. This is the Palatia site, with an ancient building with Cyclopean walls.

The road continues on to **Potamianata**. All the village's claims to fame are close to the point the road enters it: a demolished mill, a 200- to 300-year-old square cistern of the type common in this area, built on an incline to catch rainwater, and the statue of M. Antipas. Turn left from the main road and head in the direction of **Makriotika**. The lovely square with the fountain is like a balcony from which you can look out over the whole plain of Pilaros.

The entrance to the village of Potamianata

The small village of Assos on the tip of the peninsula and the sheltered harbour that separates it from the Venetian castle

Argostoli – Assos – Fiskardo

Once again, take the main road and after Siniori head towards Assos. All along the way you have a panoramic view of the delicious beach of Mirtos. Continue on in a northerly direction. The views will be adequate compensation for resisting the impulse to take the road down to Mirtos Bay. On the way you will go through **Anomeria**. From here on you are in Erissos, the northernmost section of the island. It is divided into Upper and Lower, Ano and Kato, Erissos. Kato Erissos was left relatively intact by the earthquakes. Many Neoclassical buildings still grace its villages.

A fork in the main road leads to the picturesque village of Assos, built on the neck of the enchanting peninsula of **Assos**, nestled among pines, cypresses and terraced fields. Don't be misled by the bustling town square and the modern rooms to rent. In spite of the crowds that visit it every year, Assos has kept the small-village atmosphere it had before the tourist invasion: If you climb the steps above the square you will see flower-filled courtyards and domestic animals. The village was rebuilt after the 1953 earthquakes with aid sent by the French Prime Minister Georges Bidault. Assos' tiny houses, roofed with red tiles and interspersed with ruins, extend from the hills down to the sea.

On the hilltop stands the old pink church of Agios Georgios built in 1871, with a lovely bell-tower. The villagers named the small square next to the sea Paris, out of gratitude to the French. Among the plane-tree, the palm and the poplar which shade the square stands the ancient Olive-tree, on which Cosmas the Aetolian leaned as he taught. One story goes that it was summer, and the

The ruins of the Catholic Church of Agios Markos in the Assos fortress

cicadas were so noisy that Agios Cosmas couldn't be heard, so he shouted to them to shut up ...and they did!

Undoubtedly the sight most worth seeing in Assos is the 16th-century Venetian fortress. On the unpaved road up to the fortress (where most of the villagers take a stroll in the cool evening hours) you will encounter the chapel of Panagia Plakoula. It took its name from the icon carved in relief on a stone slab, which was found on the beach below the fortress; it can be seen outside the chapel.

The idea to build the fortress dates from 1585 when the legation of the commune of Kefalonia asked the Venetian senate for a fortress to protect the islanders from attack by pirates and Turks. Construction began in 1593: The speed with which it was built indicates its importance. The position it occupied, on a peninsula, at an elevation of 170 m, where the only means of access was a narrow passage 51 m wide, made it impregnable. In addition, Assos' port was a safe natural harbour. The fortress lost its strategic importance in 1684, when the Venetians regained the fortress of Lefkada. It remained, however, the seat of the Venetian provisor until 1797.

The Assos fortress commands a view from the hilltop on the peninsula

Still standing are the vaulted semi-circular entrance-way, the walls, and in thick vegetation the ruins of the house of the provisor and those of the Catholic Church of San Marco (1604). Until 1815 the fortress housed a rural prison, because it offered no means of escape. The fortress was lived in until 1968 by the Destounis family, whose graves can be seen next to the small Church of Profitis Ilias, dating from 1889. Behind the prison is the second gate; one can also reach it from the left side of Assos. Imprison yourselves for a while in the mysterious atmosphere of the fortress and admire the unique view and the enchanting sunset.

In **Defaranata** you can say a last good-bye to the Assos peninsula. In this village there are several ruined mills, once used to grind grain. At the Liostassakia locale, 500 m north-west of the village, the archaeologist Marinatos discovered twelve rectangular rock tombs. On the same road you will come to **Kokolata**, with the Church of Agios Nikolaos, dating from 1700. The last village before you come out onto the main road again is **Kothreas**, whose inhabitants cultivate grapes and work as fishermen.

In **Enossi**, the destruction wrought by the passage of time and the earthquakes is apparent in the ruins of the Church of

The villages of Erissos on the island's interior are less tourist-oriented and more traditional

the Panagia. Enossi offers a few rooms to rent, as does **Vassilikiades**, also on the main road. From this point, the large commune of Touliata begins. On the main road you will encounter the villages of **Ventourata**, with a view out towards Ithaki and **Konidarata**, where you can see the Church of Agios Ioannis, built in 1929. A turnoff to the right leads to the villages of **Vigli**, **Tzamarelata**, with rooms to rent and masonry ovens in its well-tended gardens, and finally the big village of **Manganos**, the area's commercial centre. Here the road branches; heading downhill you will pass **Agrilias** and continue on to **Halikeri**, a village that was once the target of frequent pirate attacks. One of the formidable pirates lost his son in a battle with the villagers and buried him on the seashore, where he built the Catholic Church of Agia Ierousali. But this area is better known for the rocky white beach of Alikes or Porto Alaties, as the locals call it. It boasts indentations full of salt, where you can try a briny curative bath before retiring to the small taverna higher up for a meal of fresh fish.

The magnificent Church of the Resurrection is a gift from a wealthy Greek from Russia

After Manganos you come out again onto the main road and pass through **Steliata** and **Antipata Erissou**, the island's northernmost village. In the square stands the magnificent Church of the Resurrection, built in 1934 in the Russian style, a gift from a wealthy Greek living in Russia. From the square an unpaved road leads to the village of **Psilithrias**. Between here and Fiskardo, at the Spiliovouno locale, is the "throne of Queen Fiskarda", as the locals call it. It is a concavity 2.3 m wide and 2.4 m deep hollowed out of a rock. It was probably a place of worship or a tomb. Farther to the west there is a section of Cyclopean walls from historical times.

Another road starts out from the square towards **Markantonata**, site of the Church of Agios Spiridon.

Just before Fiskardo you will pass the long beach of Emplissi. The island's northernmost port, **Fiskardo** is a well-known anchorage for yachts. It took its name from the Norman leader Robert Guiscard, who, during his second invasion of Kefalonia, died of a heart attack on July 17, 1085 near Cape Panormos. It is said that originally he was buried there. Panormos was changed to Piskardo after Guiscard and after the 13th century it became Fiskardo. Because of a peculiarity in the underlying geological strata

Fiskardo, the island's most picturesque town, according to the English traveller Miller

here, the town was seemingly miraculously saved from the wrath of the earthquake. Fiskardo is perhaps the island's most picturesque town, as the English traveller Miller contended in the 19th century. In 1975 it was declared a traditional town protected by law from unseemly development. After leaving your car in the parking lot, you can wander through the narrow streets lined with traditional 18th-century houses, with tiled roofs and tiny balconies entwined with grapevines. Fiskardo has every amenity to offer the visitor. Its jetty has been turned into a shopping centre with tourist shops, tavernas and bars and of course fishing boats, caiques, luxury craft and speedboats. One of the traditional buildings has a mermaid holding a ship painted on its facade.

From the middle of the harbour, steps lead up to the Church of Panagia tis

Traditional buildings with paintings by anonymous folk artists now house the seaside shops

The lights from Fiskardo's shops at night make the town look like a painting by a famous artist

Platiteras. Where the church stands today there was in Byzantine times a country chapel. Around 1680 artisans from Souli built a monastery which was demolished in the earthquakes of 1767. It was rebuilt and became quite prosperous during the 19th century. The 1953 earth-quakes created the ruins visible today behind the sanctuary. An important fresco dating from 1676 has been attributed to

The 6th-century early Christian basilica on Fournias peninsula

A view of Fournias peninsula, where Palaeolithic tools were discovered

Ruins in the village of Tselentata. The islet of Daskalio can just be distinguished in the distance

K. Tzane Bounialis. Next to the Panormos Hotel, a fence encloses Roman baths and a necropolis discovered by A. Sotiriou. These ruins date from 150-200 AD, and include four carved stone sarcophagi with representations of Artemis. The sarcophagi had been desecrated, but the artefacts brought to light in the excavations (jewelry, coins, etc.) are important and enlightening. Opposite the village, on Fournias peninsula, stand the ruins of an early Christian basilica dating from the 6th century; there was possibly an ancient temple of Apollo on the same site. Recently Professor G. Kavadias discovered stone tools from the Paleolithic Era. Kavadias stresses the similarity of the inhabitants of the Fiskardo settlement to those of neighbouring Epirus, the Peloponnese and southern Italy, which proves that they were in contact with each other. According to the geographer Joseph Partsch, the ancient town was a dependency of Same.

The sea between Fiskardo and Ithaki, where the water is 165 m deep, is home to the Mediterranean Seal (Monachus monachus). Its existence was mentioned by Homer. It takes refuge in sea-caves and lives on fish and octopuses. It usually gives birth to only one pup. This likeable animal is threatened with extinction, due in part to illegal fishing practices, but mainly to the development of tourism. It is the duty of each one of us to avoid disturbing the seals and to report to the authorities anything we think may be harmful to the defenceless animals or their young.

A sick pup of the Mediterranean Seal (Monachus monachus). The cause of its disease is unknown. Could it be that the North Sea virus in conjunction with the unscrupulousness of certain fishermen is exterminating them?

Continuing on the seaside road, you encounter Foki inlet, the place the inhabitants of Fiskardo prefer to swim and moor their sailing boats. Those who would rather not return to Fiskardo for a meal can eat in the small taverna a short way up the hill. From there an uphill paved road leads to the villages of **Tzelendata**, in the midst of cypress and pine trees, and **Evreti**. The rocky islet of Asteris or Daskalio which can be seen in the distance, in the strait between Ithaki and Kefalonia, is believed to be Asteris,

The village of Plagia, built on the side of a hill

where Penelope's suitors waited for Telemachus to return from Pylos. The little Church of Ai-Nikolas was built in 1920 by the shipowner Potamianos, when one of his ships ran aground on the islet. Some experts believe that Doulihas bay, opposite Asteris, was the Dulichium mentioned by Homer.

In order to reach the rest of the villages of Erissos, you must return to Vassilikiades and leave the asphalt paved road. On a hill opposite stands **Messovounia**. The first building you encounter in the village is the earthquake-proof Lyceum built in 1933, of which the inhabitants are justly proud. On the hill stands the Church of Agia Paraskevi with a bell-tower dating from 1884. Three km further on, the passable but unpaved road brings you to **Plagia**. The bell-tower of the Church of Zoodohos Pigi on the hill is one of the island's five oldest. You might prefer to continue on the more primitive dirt road for 5 km until you come to **Vari**. On the left is the village cemetery, where the 400-year-old late Byzantine cruciform Church of Panagia Kougiana still stands. The frescoes on its interior walls were painted by a folk artist. On the left-hand side he painted hell, with scenes reminiscent of Dante's Inferno, and on the right-hand side he painted paradise. The locals, ignorant of their great importance, whitewashed over the frescoes on the right side; fortunately, the

The unique frescoes inside the Church of the Panagia Kougiana

left side has been preserved. (Ask a villager to show you around.) In the village square is the newly-built Church of Agios Stefanos, worth a visit for its marble altar-screen with Corinthian columns, a miniature version of the altar-screen in the Athens cathedral (metropolis).

From Karia an asphalt paved road leads to **Patrikata**, clinging to the hill opposite, and to **Komitata**, where each family has its own vineyard. After another 6 km, you come to **Neohori** or **Nihori**. Just below is the 16th-century Monastery of Theotokos. The ruins are the remains of the village, which was originally located close by the monastery. On the 15th of August a festival is held to celebrate the village's deliverance from a pestilence in 1200. The road now descends to Agia Efimia. Opposite the eastern shores of Kefalonia, the island of Ithaki beckons you on to long journeys and adventures.

A view of the tiny hamlet of Neohori

Flowering courtyards grace the small houses on Paliki peninsula

Argostoli – Lixouri – Katoi

This itinerary takes you to the western side of Kefalonia, taken up in its entirety by the Paliki peninsula. This is the most cultivated, and therefore the most productive part of the island. The road passes through fertile vineyards, olive orchards and melon-fields.

Many of the villages retain the names they had in antiquity. These place-names, along with the great number of archaeological finds in the area, connect it to Homer's tales, in particular with his Dulichium. This was the site of the ancient city of Paliki, Pale, which in historical times was the island's most powerful city. Strabo mentions that there was a sea between Thinea and Paliki.

In the mountain village of **Atheras** you can buy freshly-made milk products and thyme honey. In the square stands the Church of the Evangelistria whose bell-tower was built in 1933. From the square, a paved road leads to Agios Spiridon or Porto Bay, with the chapel of Agios Spiridon and a lovely beach. Just opposite, on the rocky islet of Averonissi, seagulls and other water birds make their nests.

You will pass through **Kouvalata**, a small hamlet with beautiful little houses, and then **Agios Dimitrios**. An unpaved road on your right leads down to the Ritsata locale, site of the house and lands of the great satirical poet and social reformer A. Laskaratos (1811-1901). The ruins visible today belong to a house built with the help of the poet's friends after the 1867 earthquakes destroyed the larger original house.

Laskaratos was the scion of an aristocratic Lixouri family. He went to Europe to study, returned to Lixouri and dedicated his life to writing prose and poetry. The butt of his satire was the Orthodox clergy, which he maintained consisted of crafty,

The bronze statue of Andreas Laskaratos by Aparthis in the port of Lixouri

exploiting priests, as well as the expressions of worship of a superstitious, prejudiced people. His work is also pervaded with a feeling of mistrust for the cause of the Radicals. A rationalist, obstinate in his views, he almost caused Neofitos Vamvas to renounce him as a pupil and prompted Lord Gilford to embrace him as the promise of a free man.

The small plain of Kehrion outside Lixouri took its name from Kechraeae in Corinth, of which it may have been a colony. On a turnoff to the right is the monastery of Kehrion. Its history is associated with yet another miracle wrought by the Virgin. Heavy chains have been placed around her throne, and there is an inscription giving the date, August 23, 1694, and the names Iakovos, Georgios and Ioannis.

The story is as follows: Some Kefalonians were taken prisoner by Ottoman pirates and shut up in the dungeons in Tripoli on the Barbary Coast in Africa. When the day of the Assumption of the Virgin arrived, which is the occasion of a festival in the monastery, they felt so homesick that before they went to sleep they prayed to be able to go back home. When they awoke they discovered to their great joy that they were under a bridge close to the monastery, over which the throne was carried every year in a procession. So they dedicated their chains to the Virgin. Their portraits are represented on the marble bas-relief over the entrance to the church.

Loukerata is the birthplace of the famous icon-painter Loukeris. The road continues on to **Lixouri**, capital of Paliki and the second-largest town on the island. It is on the western side of the Paliki peninsula facing the Lassi peninsula. You can reach it by driving the 33 km from Argostoli, or by ferry-boat (sailing time 25 minutes).

The farming community of Lixouri is first mentioned in 1534, in a written protest to the Venetian senate. In 1800, under the French occupation, Lixouri became the headquarters of the Bureau of Sanitation and the City Court, and this gave rise to hopes that it would become capital of the island; Argostoli had been the capital since 1759. Naturally, a vendetta started up between the two towns which lasted for centuries; a few people may still be keeping it alive today.

I believe the following hitherto unpublished note written in 1933 may be of interest. It gives a picture of the folklore and culture of Lixouri before the earthquakes:

from "The Beautiful Peasant Girl of Laskaratos":

"...At that time, Lixouri, that romantic little town, was a poor, austere, backward place. The women did not dare venture into the marketplace by day to do their shopping, so the shopping was done by the men. The women went down at sun-

The Markato, which housed Lixouri's courts, one of the works of Napier which was destroyed in 1953 (Korgialenio Museum)

October 20, 1858 – a post-earthquake picture of the procession on the feast-day of Agios Gerassimos in Lixouri (collection of G. Galanos)

set or after dark to buy what they needed from the shops. There was no electric light then, only oil lamps. And Petritsi Square had a very amiable appearance in the evenings, with its oil lamps and illuminated shops...

»...Over there was the marketplace, with its peristyle and shops. The clock struck the hours romantically, and they rolled by silently and slowly, in the little town. Every morning, the rooster of Grigoris the grocer (he was a tame rooster) would go for his stroll undisturbed in the small square. Under the square's plane-tree, the scholars and the politicians held long discussions. The Gymnasium teachers played backgammon by the coffee-shop of Karonias (Repoussis), which was the most aristocratic coffee-shop in town...

»...Swimming, the coffee-shop, people getting together and engaging in small-talk – this is the recreation of the Lixouriote. With his ironical, caustic wit, the Lixouriote finds plenty of things to talk about. That is why in one of my earlier

Even though Lixouri is the island's second-largest town, it bears little resemblance to cosmopolitan Argostoli

It is very pleasant to walk through the town's streets with their low houses and gardens replete with flowers

notes I called Lixouri the «town of five thousand tongues». And what tongues! May God steer you clear of them!! In spite of all their teasing and irony, Lixouriotes don't quarrel easily. They are happy and cheerful. In the evening in the taverna, next to a glass of Vostilidi, Thiniatiko or Havdotiko wine, they will sing their own local songs, arias and ariettas, where polyphony is indispensable.

»...The moon bathed in light, a cool north-west breeze blowing and the singer's head full of exaltation (the red wine has a little something to do with that). This is how the fine timbre and high notes come out without forcing. Serenades are often sung to certain girls, under certain small balconies and windows..."

Even Lixouri could not remain standing in battle with Enceladus. Two violent earthquakes (January 23, 1867 and August 12, 1953) completely demolished most of the old traditional houses. But don't despair when reading about all this lost beauty. Present-day Lixouri may not look anything like the larger town of Argostoli, but it boasts several important churches, lovely buildings, small traditional houses and flower-filled squares with picturesque coffee-shops. Today's tourist will find modern accommodations, tavernas, nightclubs and immaculate beaches for swimming.

The bed of the dry river that once ran through the town of Lixouri and separated it into two parts

As you enter the town, on your right stands the Lyceum building, with the fine statue of Stamos Petritsis, the work of the sculptor Bonanos. Continuing straight on, you cross one of the three bridges that once united the two sides of town. Under it is a dry river bed, which was in former times quite a rushing torrent. Among de Bosset's numerous public works was an elegant bridge, which the local wags facetiously dubbed "la Seine", just as they called Lixouri "little Paris". On the seaside road is Radicals' Square,

The statue of Stamos Petritsis, by the sculptor Bonanos

The entrance to the once famous Valianios Professional School, which escaped destruction in the earthquakes

with statues of three of the ten radical Parliamentary deputies who signed the resolution to unite the Ionian islands with Greece. But they are not the only statues to be found in the town. The Lixouriotes have honoured all their distinguished men with statues and busts, which now grace the town's squares and parks.

The bronze statue of Andreas Laskaratos, a work of Apartis, welcomes visitors arriving by sea. Between the two jetties, fishermen tie their boats and caiques. In the main square above the harbour, as you enjoy some of the local sweets, you may notice a huge poplar-tree; according to I. Tsitselis, it was planted by Lixouri's first policeman after the celebrations on the occasion of unity with Greece in 1864! Kefalonians are "masters" of sweetmeats, among them mandoles, rozolia and Lixouri's koulouria.

Most of Lixouri's public buildings were built after the 1953 earthquakes with funds donated by local benefactors. Buildings that remained standing after the quake are the mansion of Professor M. Geroulanos, the building that houses Elementary School No. 1, the Home for the Aged and the buildings of the Valianios Professional School.

Also preserved in its pre-1953 condition is the Tipaldon-Iakovaton Public Library and Museum housed in the old mansion of this prominent family. It consists of 14 rooms whose ceilings are decorated with intricate wooden latticework. In the library on the first floor, the manuscripts and books are kept, a total of 25,000 volumes, of which 7,000 were a gift from the Iakovaton family. On the second floor a collection of 36 important icons are on exhibit, including two valuable icons, one painted by the monk Filotheos Skoufos and and the other possibly by Michael Damaskinos. There are also three manuscript Gospels, bishops' robes, furniture, etc. During the first 10 days in August, theatrical and musical events are held in the mansion's forecourt (garden theatre). Another library is the Petritsios Public Library "O Damodos", near the third bridge, on the site of the old Petritsis home; it also houses an extensive collection of books.

The Church of Agios Haralambos, a

The stately Tipaldon-Iakovaton Mansion, which houses the Public Library and Museum. Among its exhibits is a manuscript on parchment dating from the 10th century

little further down the road, was built in 1754. But as Lixouri existed well before that time, it is not known just when Agios Haralambos became the town's patron saint. His reliquary was kept in a monastery in Meteora until 1952, when the Metropolitan Herouvim presented it to Lixouri.

On the patronal festival of Agios Haralambos, on February 10, a mass is held, followed by a majestic procession; with the band at its head it passes in front of the Geroulanos mansion, on the ground floor of which is the room where papa-Bassias, a local saint once lived. After wending its way past the square and the harbour, the procession winds up at the Church of Agios Gerassimos.

Agios Haralambos was a priest in Magnesia in Asia Minor. At the time of the persecution of the Christians in 198 AD, he was over 100 years old. The martyrdom he was subjected to did not for a moment diminish his faith or cause him to yield, despite his advanced age. He is believed to offer protection from various diseases. On the church's bell-tower the statuette representing the plague can still be seen. It was formerly painted red with gold eyes. Agios Haralambos is believed to have saved Lixouri from that terrible disease.

Out of Lixouri's many important churches, only frescoes and finely-worked altar-screens were saved from the catastrophic earthquakes; they have been installed in the newer Churches of Agios Nikolaos ton Xenon (1771), Taxiarhon, Agia Triada and Panagia ton Perligadon. Outside the latter, every evening between the 1st and 15th of August, three rockets are fired, culminating in a popular festival on the evening of the 15th, when the sky is illuminated by Bengal lights and the town band plays marches.

In the Church of Agios Spiridon the bones of the local saint papa-Bassias are

The Church of Agios Haralambos and the bell-tower with the sculpture representing the plague

kept. This church's important altar-screen has been moved to the chapel of Agios Andreas in Matzavinatios Hospital.

Outside the Church of Agios Nikolaos ton Miniaton stands the statue of Ilias Miniatis (1669-1714), metropolitan of Kerniki and Kalavrita, a great ecclesiastical orator.

Traditionally in competition with each other, the inhabitants of Argostoli and Lixouri have always engaged in friendly rivalry. The Paliki Philharmonic School is in no way inferior to that of Argostoli. It is the second-oldest school in Greece. It was founded in 1836 by P. Skarlatos. The travelling Italian companies of actors are the source of the town's musical tradition. Most of the repertory is taken from Italian operas. The aforementioned unpublished

The Paliki Philharmonic playing in Lixouri's main square on Good Friday (collection of G. Galanos)

note has this to say on the subject:

"...I talked before about the serenades sung in the tavernas and the narrow streets, in the Square and on the breakwater. Those popular serenades were of local, folk origin. To be sure there are also bits and pieces of old Italian operas which were later turned into serenades, after being altered or even corrupted. Every Lixouriote knows at least one aria from an opera. And he sings it whenever he wants, whenever he feels like it. On the street, at home, in the taverna..."

North of the present-day town, on Douris Hill or Paleokastro, stood the ancient city of Pale. In historical times, Pale was the island's most powerful city. It was also the first port of call for the Corinthians in their commerce with Sicily. That is the reason for the strong friendship between the two cities, as can be seen in their similar religious beliefs. Pale had a navy of some consequence and took part in several wars. It was often the target of conquerors, due to its geographic position and the fertility of its soil. Not much archaeological excavation has been carried out in the area. Pale's coins bear a representation of Cephalus, Procris and Pegasus on one side and an ear of wheat or a dolphin on the other. Examples of them are on exhibit in the Archaeological Museum in Argostoli.

Holiday-makers in Lixouri will not have to go far to find a beach: Agios Spiridon beach has shallow water safe for small children. Another beach, this one south of Lixouri, is **Lepeda**, with reddish sand and a dark-coloured rock in the middle. Here you can play beach volley or walk to the monastery/cave of Agia Paraskevi. From the evidence that has come down to us, we are informed that the cave began to be used in 1568 as a church. Around 1668 a monk turned it into a monastery for monks. In the cave to the right of the church, St. Anthimos Kourouklis lived as a hermit. After the earthquakes in 1767 it was abandoned.

St. Anthimos Kourouklis was born in 1727. He was stricken by smallpox at the age of 7 and lost his sight; he regained it in his right eye only, due to his mother's prayers and profound faith. After the earthquakes, he came to the monastery and turned it into a nunnery. He lived as a hermit in the cave next to the church. He left this earthly life in 1781 and was buried in the monastery. When he was pronounced a saint, his bones were divided up among the faithful.

Today the monastery and cave have been abandoned, but you can see the old gate and the demolished interior. Since 1920 the monastery has been a dependency of the monastery of Agios Gerassimos. As you are leaving, be sure to notice the terra cotta-tiled roof of the old church!

The area south of Lixouri is called Katoi by the locals. A turnoff to the left from the main road will lead you to the village of **Mihalitsata** which commands a view of the olive orchards and the fields. In the village of **Soulari** stands the church of Agia Marina surrounded by cypresses. It houses marvellous icons by T. Poulakis and I. Moshos. Over the entrance there is a bas relief of Agia Marina, with knights' coats-of-arms to the left and right of it. An unpaved road on the right leads to the splendid beach known as Mia Lakko, with fine red sand and deep blue water.

The next village you come to on the main road is **Mantzavinata**, famous for the fine frescoes in the Churches of Agios Spiridon, Panagia and Agia Sofia; the latter is being restored to its former appearance. A narrower road starts from Mantzavinata and winds up at the developed beach of Xi, which is essentially a continuation of the long beach starting at Mia Lakko. Here the sea is quite warm and shallow and therefore suitable for

The large developed beach of Xi, with red sand and shallow water

The entrance to the Church of the Panagia in the village of Soulari

Mia Lakko beach and the rocky islet of Vardiani, a good place to fish

The dolphin mosaic from the temple of Poseidon in Vatsa

children. Opposite lies the regularly-shaped rocky islet of Vardiani, a paradise for amateur fishermen.

The main road winds up at Akrotiri, site of Kounopetra, one of the island's strange geological phenomena. It is a massive rock a few centimetres from the shoreline that at one time used to move rhythmically. Kounopetra is the rock directly in front of a bench with a square cement slab on it.

Investigations which began on Kounopetra in 1953 never reached a conclusion. The physicist and mathematician E.T. Konstandakatos had described the phenomenon in 1900 as follows:

"A large monolithic rock, 20 paces in circumference, a short distance from the water, moves uninterruptedly in an east-to-west direction. Its gentle movement is visible from the shore, but whoever stands on it can also feel the rock's pulsating motion. It makes 20 vacillations a minute. Before the earthquake of 1867, the rock almost touched the shore and visitors placed a knife between them which would be pressed against it, but after the earthquake the gap widened..."

All this came to an end after 1953, when the rock stopped rocking. The earthquakes shifted sections of the seabed, stabilising its base. Today's visitors stand on it, and perhaps deep down they hope it will start moving again!

Vouni is the birthplace of the sculptor G. Bonanos; it is also the site of the Mantzavinos Winery. **Havriata** is a village built on a hill, with a breathtaking view out over the sea. Standing on another hill is the restored Church of the Panagia, with beautiful old frescoes and a carved wooden altar-screen. The philosopher Vikentios Damodos (1700-1752) was from Havriata; he founded one of Kefalonia's first schools in 1721.

At the locale known as Plati-Boros, among pines and orange-trees, lie the ruins of the villa of the historian Ilias Tsitselis (1850-1927), author of "Kefalonian Miscellany". His archives have been preserved in perfect condition in the home of his grandson in Lixouri. To the left of the village a narrow dirt road leads to Gerogombo beacon, whose beacon shines as far as the village at night. At the chapel of Agios Nikolaos in the Vatsa area, there was an ancient temple of Poseidon with a dolphin mosaic (now in the Argostoli Archaeological Museum). Nearby is Potamos beach, with red sand.

Just before Havdata, an unpaved but passable road leads to the two oldest monasteries in Paliki. As you descend toward the sea you can see on your right-hand side the ruins of the **Monastery of Agia Paraskevi Tafion or Tafii**. It stands on the site of the ancient city of Taphus, which took its name from the island's first king Taphius and the Teleboans or Taphians.

A five minutes' drive beyond it brings you to the **Kipoureon Monastery**, clinging to the edge of the rock. On the spot where the bell-tower now stands, a monk from the Tafii Monastery originally built a hut and began to cultivate the land. In 1759, the Archimandrite of Paxi, H. Petropoulos, built the church. The monastery was demolished in the earthquakes, and in 1964 only the church was rebuilt. It was slightly damaged in 1915 when the crew of a French battleship saw the smoke from the monastery's chimney and thought it was an enemy ship. Today the cells are being rebuilt and the monastery is regaining its pre-earthquake appearance, as you may ascertain from the old photographs in the guests' quarters. In the monastery's church you will see post-Byzantine icons and important relics. This route is not recommended only for the religiously-inclined: The scenery is unique and anyone who fails to see it has missed something special in Kefalonia. In the stone-paved courtyard by the well, or under the grapevine with a view of the sea, a monk will offer visitors coffee and pure honey from his beehives. Near Kipouria is a cave 40 m deep known as Drakospilia. A shepherd willing to leave his herd for a while will be happy to show it to you.

Havdata, the main village of Paliki, offers restaurants and tavernas. In the splendid old Church of Agii Apostoli you can see many post-Byzantine icons dating from 1890, important frescoes and a carved and gilded wooden altar-screen which dates from 1730. From the church's courtyard there is an excellent view of the village.

The Monastery of Kipoureon is considered to be one of the best places on the island to watch the sunset

Argostoli – Lixouri – Anogi

The northern part of the Paliki peninsula is called Anogi by the locals. From the picturesque windmill “tou Latsi” some of its villages can be seen. You can reach Anogi by taking the road that follows the dry Lixouri river-bed. The 14th-century nunnery of the **Assumption of the Virgin**, **Agion Apostolon Koronatou** was built on the spot where an icon of the Virgin was found, a copy of which can be seen on the throne. The Virgin shed tears during the 1867 earthquakes, and those tears can still be seen! The lovely icons on the altar-screen were dedicated by a priest in the monastery who was miraculously cured of an illness when he was a child. But the icon of the Assumption to the left of the chancel was brought here by some families from Koroni in the Peloponnese. The nunnery has guests' quarters.

You pass through **Favatata** and **Mandoukata** and turn up to the left towards the mountain village of **Kaminarata**, which boasts a folk dance troupe famous both in Greece and abroad. The road, shaded by cypresses, comes to **Rifi** and continues to the beautiful village of **Damoulianata**, with its Church of the Panagia. In **Agia Thekli**, ask to see the old church of the same name and the two-story Neoclassical G. Livieratos building above the road. The latter has been used as a Gymnasium since the earthquakes. As you leave the village the last things you see are the ruins of the small Church of Archangeli. Below Agia Thekli lie four villages drenched in greenery. To the right at the intersection is **Kalata**, where citrus- and other fruit is cultivated. We continue on the same road to **Skineas**, with the Church of the Presentation of the Virgin, which was destroyed by the earthquakes and rebuilt in 1961.

The inland villages of Paliki, or Anogi as the locals call it

Another road leads to **Monopolata**. Here you can visit the old Church of Agia Paraskevi, with a finely carved wooden altar-screen. As you leave the village, you will see a narrow dirt road that leads to the small Church of the Panagia ton Rongon. Its interior is being restored to its former appearance, but its splendid Baroque facade remains. A turnoff to the right brings you to **Delaportata**, a small quaint village built on a hill. Near it are the sulphurous healing waters of Agia Eleoussa.

Back at the intersection, continue on straight ahead to **Vilatoria**. There you will find the second of the island's two biggest and best beaches, Petani, with white sand and deep blue water. The locals call it “Xouras (Old Geezer) beach”, after the old man who opened the first small seaside taverna there. He is no longer living, but you can still enjoy a meal of fresh fish or other seafood. In **Vovikes**, see the old private chapel of Agia Irini at the side of the road.

The main road winds up in **Kondogenada**, a village built like an amphitheatre on the side of a hill. In its churches you will have an opportunity of admiring many post-Byzantine icons. In 1930 at the Ikopeda locale, a Mycenean pit-tomb came to light. Shortly thereafter, in 1933, in the area of the little valley of Halikias at the edge of the village, three post-Mycenean tombs were found, hollowed out of the limestone common in this area and surrounded by cypress-trees.

Not to be Missed

Kefalonia is the largest of the Ionian islands, and sixth in size of all the Greek islands. It is of interest from an archaeological, cultural, geological and touristic standpoint. Because of its large area, its many villages with their churches, beaches and strange phenomena, I am unable to convey the special beauty of each of them in a few pages.

To those of you on a tight schedule who want to see the most representative sights, I would suggest the following: Argostoli with its museums and ancient Crane; the Monastery of Agios Gerassimos, the fortress of Agios Georgios and the tombs in Mazarakata; Skala; Poros and the royal tomb; the Ainos fir forest; Same, Drongarati and the other caves, Karavomilos and Melissani lake; Agia Efimia; picturesque Assos with its Venetian fortress; traditional Fiskardo; Lixouri, the Tipaldon-Iakovaton Public Library and Museum and the monasteries of Paliki.

In trying to select the best beaches on an island famous above all for its beaches, you might be well advised not to miss: Makris Gialos and Platis Gialos, Avithos, Spartia, Lourdas, Skala, Poros, Antissamos, Mirtos, Petani and Xi.

Of course, all these things are only a part of this wonderful island, and I don't believe they can give you a complete picture of it. I also believe that, if you are not able to extend your stay beyond what you had originally planned, you will surely promise yourself to return as your ship sails away and the island's shores are lost from sight...

Petani beach, the most famous beach on the Paliki peninsula and one of the island's finest

The small rocky island of Ithaki is washed by the tranquil blue-green waters of the Ionian Sea

Ithaki

With an area of 96 square kilometres, Ithaki is the fifth largest of the Ionian islands. It lies south of Lefkada, east of Kefalonia, from which it is separated by a channel 3-4 km wide, and west of the Ehinades islands.

It is a mountainous island, whose highest peak is Mt. Niritos at 800 m. Its coast is rocky and lined with sand and pebble beaches washed by blue-green water.

The island's economy is based on fishing, its choice quality olive oil and wine, and tourism. Many Ithacans are still sailors or emigrants living abroad.

Ithaki, a universal symbol of nostalgia and love for one's place of birth, is a small paradise on earth. In former times, many "lords" and "archaeologists" visited it. In recent years, other travellers have discovered its beauties and prefer it to the larger, more frequented Ionian islands.

Ithaki can be reached from Kefalonia's eastern ports on the eastern side of Kefalonia (Sami-Pisso Aetos and Agia Efimia-Vathi). You can get around the island on the local bus, in taxis or rented vehicles. Tourist agencies organise excursions by bus or caique to the island's villages and beaches.

Mythology

Ithaki (ancient Ithaca) is said to have taken its name from the island's first settler, Ithacus, son of Poseidon and Amphimele. When he and his brothers, Neritus and Polyctor, grew up, they came to live on the island. Another myth has it that Ithacus was the son of Pterelaus and grandson of Taphius. Other experts believe the name is from the Phoenician "Utica" (distant colony) or "Ithys" (cheerful, frank). The island's conquerors gave it various names, such as Nericie, Val de Compare (Valley of the Godfather), Fiaki and finally Thiaki.

Its most important hero, however, was not Ithacus, but resourceful Odysseus, the most popular character in Greek mythology and one of the most famous and best-loved heroes in Homer's epics. Homer was a mythographer, and thus what he conveys lies somewhere between myth and reality.

Hermes and Chione, a nymph of snowy Mt. Parnassus, had a son, Autolycus, who as he grew up proved himself adept at stealing and breaking oaths. At the same time another wily shepherd, Sisyphus, used to graze his sheep next to those of Autolycus. One would steal the other's sheep, until Autolycus was defeated in a contest of trickery. Then he got the idea that a son born to his daughter Anticleia and Sisyphus would inherit both his parents' cunning. Sisyphus, impatient to lie down with the fair maiden, didn't wait until his wedding night. Laertes asked for Anticleia's hand in marriage, when she had already become pregnant by Sisyphus (tragedies of Aeschylus, Sophocles and Euripides).

Another myth says that Odysseus was the lawful son of Laertes and Anticleia, and that he was born in a cave on Mt. Niritos because it was raining. Autolycus named his grandson Odysseus, that is, hated by everyone (as Homer interprets it in the *Odyssey)*. After he grew up, he visited his grandfather on Mt. Parnassus, where his knee was injured during a wild boar hunt. Odysseus was sure Helen of Troy was going to choose him for a husband. But she chose Menelaus, and Odysseus took Penelope, daughter of Icarius and Periboea or Polycaste.

In the beginning, Odysseus did not want to take part in the Trojan War, but he was finally forced to. He fought heroically and revealed his crafty, resourceful character, particularly in the ruse of the Trojan horse, which brought about the fall of Troy. But his adventures were not over when the war ended, because he had by that time provoked the wrath of several gods. The winds blew him to Thrace, where he overcame Ismarus. From there he headed south, to the Land of the Lotus-Eaters, where whoever ate the fruit of the lotus wanted to stay. Then he sailed to northern Sicily and the land of the Cyclopes. The Cyclopes were terrible man-eating giants with one eye in the middle of their foreheads. One of them, Polyphemus, son of Poseidon, would have eaten Odysseus and his men, if Odysseus had not got him drunk and blinded him. By clinging to the underbellies of the giant's sheep, the prisoners tricked Polyphemus and escaped. This enraged Poseidon, and from that point on he was behind everything bad that befell Odysseus.

On the island of Aeolus, the god gave Odysseus the sack containing the winds; his curious companions, however, let loose the bad winds which blew them straight to the land of the man-eating Laestrygonians. Only one of Odysseus' ships was saved, which reached the island of Aeaea, where Circe lived. She was a sorceress who turned passing sailors into swine. When his companions didn't return to the ship, Odysseus went to see Circe himself. Hermes revealed her secret to him, and, after saving his companions, he stayed on the island for a month and had Telegonus by her. In the Land of the Cimmerians, the blind prophet Teiresias foresaw his future. Odysseus' next adventure took place near the island of the Sirens – women above the waist and birds below. With their superb singing they caused ships to run against the rocks and then ate the sailors. Odysseus stopped up the ears of his companions and tied himself to the mast. Then he passed the monsters Scylla and Charybdis who caused storms and devoured shipwrecked sailors. Odysseus' men persuaded him to put in at the island of Thrinacia. Unfavourable winds kept them there until some of them were so hungry that they slaughtered the sacred cattle of the Sun, who sank their ship, and only Odysseus survived. He landed on the island of Calypso, where he remained for years, until Zeus took pity on him and ordered Calypso to let him go. He built a wooden raft and after suffering Poseidon's wrath once again, he was washed up on the island of the hospitable Phaeacians. He stayed with them for a short time and finally made it home to Ithaca. There Athena transformed him into a beggar and he went to his palace, where certain noblemen, the so-called suitors of Penelope, were now living and squandering his wealth while they waited for her to choose one of them to marry. But she kept using various ruses to postpone making a decision. Odysseus appeared at the appropriate moment and killed them.

Homer's tale ends here, but tradition

A black-figure lekythos dating from 500 BC, from Eretria: Odysseus passing the Sirens (National Archaeological Museum, Athens)

has given us two versions of Odysseus' death: one, that the relatives of the suitors forced him to leave the island, and he died in Tyrrenia in Italy at an advanced age, and the other that Teiresias' prophecy was fulfilled; Odysseus had to appease Poseidon by taking a well-made oar and going to a country where the people would ask him what it was he was carrying. There he was to sacrifice to Poseidon and then return home, but death would finally come to him on the sea. With regard to his death, Eugamon the Cyrenaean said that he dreamt his son would kill him, so he decided to exile Telemachus to Kefalonia. But his other son, Telegonus, arrived and plundered and ravaged the land until Odysseus tried to stop him. Telegonus killed his father with a spear tipped with a poisoned fish-bone.

The Olympian gods, particularly Athena, Hera, Apollo and his sister Artemis, were worshipped in Ithaki.

History

Ithaki was first inhabited in 4000-3000 BC. Information about its first inhabitants, who were indigenous Greeks, comes from shards incised with the Linear A script found in Pilikata. Finds from the Pilikata settlement and Loizos Cave date back as far as 3000-2000 BC. By 1500 BC, the whole island was inhabited. The island's civilisation reached a high point in 1000 BC, when the kingdom of Ithaca included the other Ionian islands and part of the coast of Acarnania. The decline that followed was mainly due to exhaustion of the soil. The northern part of the island, however remained inhabited and under cultivation. After 180 BC Ithaki was part of the Roman province of Illyria.

Later its port town, Polis or Jerusalem, was built; Anna Comnene refers to it in her "Alexias". The port was gradually abandoned and sank into the sea after the earthquake in 967 AD. In 1086 the first pirates appeared on the scene. In 1185, Ithaki was conquered by the Normans, who ceded it in 1200 to the Orsini family. The Orsinis remained rulers of the island until 1357, when the king of Naples handed it over to the Tocco family. The Turks sacked Ithaki, along with the rest of the Ionian islands, in 1479. Material damage was tremendous, many hostages were sold as slaves and those remaining abandoned the island. When war broke out between the Turks and the Venetians in 1499, Ithaki, sharing the fate of neighbouring Kefalonia, was signed over in a treaty to the Venetians. The Venetian senate, concerned about the reduction in population due to fear of pirates and the Turks, granted lands to anyone who would come back, and exempted them from taxation. Many peo-

An old map of Ithaki

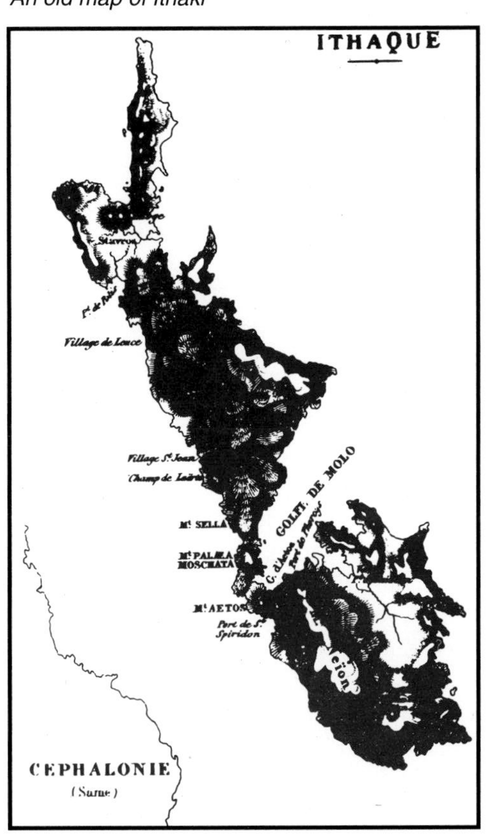

An engraving of the harbour of Ithaki in 1817 (J. Cartwright, 1789-1829)

ple were attracted by this offer, most of them from mainland Greece, which was suffering under the Turkish yoke.

In 1569 Ithaki was fortified for the first time. But the Venetian governors, taking advantage of the people's poverty and ignorance, often acted unjustly and sometimes committed acts of violence, so that the Venetian senate turned the administration of the island over to two of the local elders. During the last years of the Venetian occupation, the island's population had reached 10,000! The dawn of the 17th century found Ithaki's land under cultivation; the island had also put together a commercial fleet that was carrying on trade with Europe. This fleet took part in all the battles for freedom from the Turks up to 1821.

In 1798, the democratic French took over the Ionian islands but held them for only a year. Despite the heavy taxes they levied, their new revolutionary ideas were conveyed to the islanders. The Russians and Turks succeeded the French and a 14-member senate governed democratically until 1807. French rule returned for another two years, and in 1809 the English occupied the Ionian Islands and formed the "United States of the Ionian Islands".

During the Revolution of 1821, the Ithaki islanders joined the Friendly Society, taking part in its activities and offering a place of refuge to fugitive Greeks. It was in Galatsi in Romania that Ithacans first began the Revolution in 1821. Two waves of emigration, one in 1829 and the other in 1845, made the Ithacans famous as sailors and merchants abroad. Union with Greece in 1864, of which T. Paizis and the Radical Party were strong supporters, came at a time when Ithaki was a significant power, both in commerce and shipping.

Like the whole Ionian area, Ithaki has been stricken by repeated earthquakes. According to Partsch, the most violent occurred in 1648. There were other earthquakes in 1766, 1867 and between 1912 and 1918. Extensive devastation was caused by the 1953 earthquake.

On May 1, 1941 the Italian annexation began, and on September 24, 1943 saw the beginning of the German occupation, which lasted only a year.

Vathi, as seen from the bell-tower of the Monastery of the Kathara. The islets of Lazaretto and Skart-soumbonissi can be seen in the distance

Vathi

From the 16th century on, **Ithaki** or **Vathi** has served as the island's capital. It is the largest town on the island, built like an amphitheatre above a natural horse-shoe-shaped harbour, on the innermost point of an enclosed bay. With mountains all around it, the oddly-shaped harbour forces ships to make two left turns to get into port.

The oldest find from the area of the town is an ancient inscription indicating the existence of a temple of Artemis, but no organised settlement. Tombs were also discovered dating from Roman times.

During the Roman and Byzantine eras, there were settlements in Stouvies and Rizes, but under the Venetians their populace moved to Petaleiko hill, to get away from the pirates, who had taken up permanent residence on the coasts. With the end of the Venetian occupation, the islanders routed the pirates and built ships; trade began to flourish. In the period before 1944, the Ithacans, famed as experienced sailors and still in great demand by shipping companies even today, owned over 200 commercial ships, large and small, which sailed all over the world. That was when public and private schools were built, along with important

"To the Ithacan sailors asleep forever beneath the waves"

The beauty of Ithaki cannot be hidden even at night, when the first lights go on

churches and monasteries.

At the entrance to the harbour lies Lazaretto islet, with the chapel of the Saviour. Quarantine facilities built here during Venetian times (1668) were used until 1836 by the Venetians and English. After union with Greece they were converted into a jail for long-term prisoners (1864-1930), and were finally demolished in the earthquakes. Standing guard over the harbour entrance are two small fortresses built in 1805, remnants of the second French protectorate: to the left is Kastro, and to the right Loutsa, with ruins and cannons.

Under the English occupation, Vathi's houses were built in the Renaissance and Neoclassical styles, and the town received its water from the Merovigli aqueduct. Foundations were laid for construction of the seaside road and the wharf. Up to the beginning of the 20th century, shipping was a growing concern and much wealth was amassed in Vathi. But the wrath of Enceladus has not left many reminders of that era standing: one fine building that was lost was the best commercial navy school in the Balkans built in 1905 with funds donated by Otto and Athena Stathatos; it was the work of the architect E. Ziller. From 11,406 at the turn of the century, the island's population dwindled to 7,527 in 1951, chiefly due to emigration.

Vathi was always the administrative, cultural and economic centre of the island; witness the "Odysseus" Insurance Company founded by S.A. Ferentinos in 1858 and still in existence. The modern town was rebuilt on the old foundations and was electrified in 1927! In 1978 it was declared a landmark protected from unseemly development: every new building must harmonise with the whole. Vathi gets its water from rain-water cisterns and desalinated sea-water.

The Archaeological Museum (opening hours 8:30-2:30) exhibits Mycenean and

The town's Cultural Centre which houses a library containing rare books

The Cathedral of Ithaki (the Presentation of the Virgin), built in 1580

Classical artefacts from the excavations in Aetos, including Corinthian pottery, tools, jewelry and of course coins. To the right stands the Cultural Centre built in 1957, donated by Stathatos. It includes a hall for theatre and cinema as well as an interesting library containing rare books. There you will have the opportunity to see a rare edition of the *Odyssey* and *Iliad* in Japanese published in 1600! There are also a weighty tome of Strabo published in 1533 and the Complete Works of Agios Athanassios. In the historical archives there are documents dating from 1800.

The Cathedral (1580) houses a fine altar-screen made by craftsmen from Metsovo. In the Vounaki quarter, in the Church of the Taxiarhi, is an icon of Christ being dragged up to the cross, believed to be an early work of El Greco.

You can get a taste of old Ithaki from the Sirmis and Gratsos mansions, the pre-earthquake Stathatos home and the Neoclassical mansion of G. Drakoulis, with an artificial lake and Ionic column

The façade of the Neoclassical mansion of G. Drakoulis with its Ionic columns

The house where the hero of the Greek Revolution of 1821 Odysseas Androutsos grew up

Vathi is a traditional town and its buildings retain their traditional style of architecture

capitals, a work of the architect Tsigaras. The G. Karavias home was built after the earthquake, and the Vlassopoulos home before. You can also see the houses where the hero of the 1821 Revolution, Odysseas Androutsos, was born and grew up.

Ithaki is just as art-loving as neighbouring Kefalonia. Since 1975 the municipality has been organising various cultural events in Vathi and other villages around the island. Odyssean festivals, theatrical and musical productions and exhibitions by artists from all over Greece draw out Ithaki's crowds of art-lovers, so why not come along, too? You will be even luckier if your visit happens to coincide with some saint's-day celebrations. Then you will hear the band of the Ithacans' Artistic Association play in the town square or in one of the island's villages. Every four years since 1981, the Centre for Odyssean Studies has held an International Congress on the Odyssey in Vathi, where archaeologists and experts on Homer from all over the world gather.

The town offers hotels, rooms to rent, restaurants and bars. In the bay area, you can swim at Tsirimbis and Loutsa. Also, outside Vathi, there are several lovely inlets with sandy beaches and sky-blue water. Along the seaside road you will encounter Skinos, Filiatro and Sarakiniko.

Buses and caiques connect Vathi to the small villages around the island.

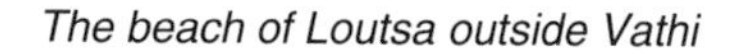

The beach of Loutsa outside Vathi

Vathi – Perahori

Using Vathi as a base, you can set out on a tour of the island's villages. First you will be visiting the eastern side, the greenest part of the island where the land slopes down gently to the coastline. From Vathi, one unpaved road leads to Marathias plateau 7 km away. From there a footpath descends to a lovely beach opposite Pera Pigadi islet.

Before saying anything further, I must warn you that for the last hundred years or so efforts to pinpoint the site of Homer's Ithaca have continued uninterrupted. In accordance with where cities were situated in Homer's time, and on the basis of Homer's topography, various archaeologists have recognised places mentioned by Homer and have formulated theories. Some archaeologists have placed Arethusa spring just above this beach at the base of the rock Petra Coracos. Coracus, the *Odyssey* tells us, fell from this rock while hunting and was killed. When his mother, Arethusa, learned of his death, her grief was such that she hanged herself on the same spot. Close by, at the Elliniko locale, what are believed to be the remains of Odysseus' pig-sties and the hut of his faithful swineherd, Eumaeus, were discovered. The excavations in the Elliniko locale, where there was a small settlement, have brought to light important Mycenean-era artefacts. At the Agios Milianos site there are a necropolis and traces of the Coracopetraeae quarter dating from the Roman era. Now you can return to Vathi and take the road which ascends Petaleiko hill to the castle and the chapel of Agios Andreas; from here the view is spell-binding. After 3 km, the road winds up in the village of **Perahori**, at an elevation of 300 m. Under the Venetians, the village had a population of about 1000, but now only 450 people are left, most of them farmers. The main product is wine, but now that the population is smaller, less is produced. Nevertheless, Perahori is still Ithaki's No. 1 wine village, and the Wine Festival at the end of August is cel-

The village of Perahori, clinging to Petaleiko Hill, with a fine view of the sea

Little tavernas with a view of the sea serve local specialties and wine

ebrated with music and dancing. On the roofs of the small tavernas on the fringe of the village overlooking the bay, the local specialty, “tserepato”, is served. It consists of meat roasted on coals in a clay pot and is best accompanied by the local wine. In the village cemetery stands the ruined Church of the Assumption of the Virgin. Its carved wooden altar-screen has been transferred to the Church of Agios Raphael in Perahori.

From here a narrow footpath leads to the island's old capital, **Paliohora** or **Epano horio**. Under the Venetians this was the most densely populated part of the island. Among its ruins one can distinguish battlements, demolished houses and roofless churches with fine Byzantine frescoes – a different world. The defensive architecture will give you the impression you are in a castle. The village's houses were built of stone and wood, with simple doorways, small windows and no balconies. Each had its own storeroom entered from the inside and its own cistern of rain-water collected from the terra cotta tiled roof. From all this we might surmise that the relations between the inhabitants were not exactly friendly! This system was also a better way of dealing with the pirate menace. Around the middle of the 16th century, a gradual movement of the population towards the coast took place, and Vathi was created. The inhabitants who stayed behind made up the population of Perahori.

From the south-western part of the ruined village, a dirt road on which a four-wheel-drive vehicle is probably necessary leads to the old **Monastery of Taxiarhi**. The 3 km drive is unique, with a view out over the fertile Marathias plateau and southern Ithaki. The monastery was built in 1645 at an elevation of 510 m and remained in use until the beginning of the 20th century. It was completely demolished in the earthquakes, however. Every year on May 1, a festival is held to celebrate the Saints' day.

Just west of the village is Ithaki's unique forest, Afentikos Longos, which supplies the inhabitants of the nearby villages with timber. The unpaved road continues on to the more arable land in the southern part of the island, with some olive and citrus orchards, but chiefly vineyards.

The lovely Church of the Dormition of the Virgin surveys the whole village from on high

Byzantine frescoes in a roofless church in the ruined medieval town of Paliohora

Vathi – Marmarospilia – Pisso Aetos

The road starts from Vathi and runs along the coast to Pisso Aetos. This is an unforgettable route, with northern Ithaki spread out before us.

Just before Dexa inlet, take the unpaved road up to Petaleiko. From here you must leave your vehicle and climb up the narrow footpath. Below you, Skartsoumbonissi islet lies like a jewel in the sea. At an elevation of 190 m is the **Cave of the Nymphs (Naiads)** or **Marmarospilia**. You will have realised by this time that we are again referring to the Odyssey and to the cave where Odysseus hid the gifts from the king of the Phaeacians, Alcinous. The cave has two entrances (a southern one for the gods and a northern one – the one you will use – for mortals!). Through a narrow passage, down steep stairs, you will enter the pit-cave, 10 m deep, with a rich array of stalactites. Excavations carried out in 1805 by Vollgraff brought to light pottery and clay figurines. In about the middle of the cave, under a marble base which probably supported the statue of a god, there is a hole in the ground. It is said that amateur archaeologists put a rooster into just such a hole, and he appeared later on Dexa beach!

On **Dexa** beach, you may lie on the very spot where the Phaeacians set down sleeping Odysseus, because some experts consider it to be the Homeric harbour of Phorcys, site of the temple of the god Phorcys (a sea-demon) and the place where Odysseus landed. Another cave north of the beach which according to William Gell was the real Cave of the Nymphs, was eroded by the sea and later destroyed by the locals, who were unaware of its historic significance. Near here is the island's only campsite.

Aetos took its name either from the two nearby hills that look like the wings of an eagle (aetos) or from the mythical city of Aedus, the small settlement lying along the bay, just above the beach of the same name. This neck of land connecting northern and southern Ithaki is the island's narrowest point with a minimum width of just 620 m. The archaeologist P. Kalligas discovered a Doric column capital in the demolished chapel of Agios Georgios. It probably originally came from an ancient temple and was later used as a pedestal for the chapel's altar. The famous archaeologist Heinrich Schliemann placed Odysseus' town here.

A visit to Mt. Aetos has for the past two centuries been an effort on the part

The entrance to the Cave of the Nymphs, small but of great historical significance

Dexa beach, the island's biggest and most frequented

Dexa Bay may once have welcomed Odysseus, tormented by years of adventures

of experienced archaeologists and other visitors to link what they see to Homer's descriptions of Odysseus' Ithaca. During the time the English were masters of Ithaki, it, along with neighbouring Kefalonia, suffered a spate of illegal excavations.

In Pisso Aetos, 4 km from Vathi on Paleokastro hill, de Bosset excavated tombs in the Hellenistic cemetery which extends up to the foot of the acropolis. His finds, mainly coins, are today in a Swiss museum.

Standing guard over the entrance to Dexa Bay is the islet of Skartsoumbonissi

In 1806, Gell claimed to have found Odysseus' ancient city on the crest of the hill, because three seas are visible from there. In 1900 the Dutch archaeologist A. Goekoop, together with the archaeologist and architect W. Dörpfeld, began to excavate, and in 1904 they found some clay figurines.

More systematic and productive excavations were carried out by the British School of Archaeology in 1930-40. Be all that as it may, the locals have always called the acropolis 300 m above sea-level on the hilltop "Odysseus' Castle". A Cyclopean wall, built in three stages from the 7th century BC on, surrounds the remains of an important settlement dating from historical times and a sanctuary dating from the end of the 9th century, dedi-

The sheltered Bay of Pisso Aetos is used by ferry-boats, swimmers and fishing enthusiasts

cated either to Apollo or to his sister, Artemis. The Cyclopean wall also encloses the Mycenean tomb excavated by Schliemann. This may be the 8th-century BC city of Alalcomenae mentioned by Plutarchus. Or it may be Aristotle's "City of the Ithacesians". Some of the 4th- and 3rd-century coins bear the helmeted head of Athena and others Odysseus wearing a cap on one side and on the other side the inscription "ITHA" or "ITHAKON". This city was abandoned during Roman times and its inhabitants relocated in Vathi.

The acropolis standing on the peak of Pisso Aetos Hill has been a source of much contention during the last two centuries about its identity

In Pisso Aetos bay, ferry-boats have taken the place of the motor-propelled caiques that once linked Ithaki to Kefalonia. The small harbour is also used by swimmers and of course fisherman, as it is a well-known fishing ground.

The so-called "field of Laertes" is still used as grazing land today

Vathi – Stavros – Frikes – Kioni

This itinerary again leads us over the narrow Aetos isthmus, and then runs up towards the north. The chapel of Agios Konstantinos is, according to some experts, built on the site of Laertes' field, where Odysseus met his father after the murder of the suitors. You can see Laertes' olive-tree, with a circumference of 18 m, said to be 2000 years old. In Hordaki, the remains of a medieval settlement were found. Take the turnoff on the right and at the Agros locale, take the road that runs up Mt. Niritos. After 6 km, you come to the **Monastery of the Kathara**, at about 600 m above sea level. It is dedicated to the Panagia Kathariotissa, protectress of the island. It is not known when the church was built, but the monastery came into use in 1696. During the 1821 Revolution it was used as a hospital for the wounded. The entrance to the monastery is reminiscent of a castle. Worthy of admiration are the altar-screen and the important icon "Birth of the Virgin", said to have been painted by St. Luke. It belonged to Epirote shepherds, who were expelled by the Turks and came here to live. In their haste, they forgot to bring the icon with them, but it came all by itself! And for those left unimpressed by all this, there is always a splendid view from the monastery's bell-tower, from which Vathi and the harbour can be seen. The monastery holds a festival every year on September 8 with local dances and music.

From the imposing bell-tower of the Monastery of the Kathara there is a splendid view of Ithaki and its harbour

Many traditions are associated with this monastery. An ancient temple of Artemis or Athena is said to have stood where the monastery stands today. It is believed that the monastery took its name from the kathara or katharidia, dry weeds that grow in the area. The peasants were burning these weeds to clear off the land when they found the icon of the Virgin. Another legend has it that it was built by followers of the Catholic Catherist sect. In 1823, Lord Byron stayed here on his way from Kefalonia to Messolongi and a mass was read in honour of the great philhellene.

From Kathara, an asphalt-paved road runs for 4 km up to the mountain village of **Anogi** or **Anoi**. Itineraries running through thick greenery are not the only

The Byzantine frescoes and the Venetian bell-tower of the Church of the Dormition of the Virgin in the village of Anogi

ones to be enjoyed. This one, for example, passes between natural rock formations and green powder-puff bushes, and provides us with a view of the whole eastern coast of Ithaki. And despite the lack of forests, it is one of the most pleasant drives to be taken on the island. You will find this out for yourselves if you make a stop to take a look at the scenery.

Anogi is one of the island's oldest villages; it was the second most important town in the Middle Ages. The village's name, which means "at the top of the world", refers to its location (at an elevation of 500 m). When the pirates moved away from the coast, the town's peasant population relocated in Stavros and in Kioni. The latter had 1000 inhabitants a century ago, and now has 100. But its population is trebled on August 14 every year for the picturesque festival in honour of the Virgin, held in the restored 12th-century Byzantine Church of the Assumption of the Virgin. There are fine 15th- and 16th-century icons on its altar-screen which extends out of the wall and was not destroyed in the earthquakes. There are clay pitchers built into the interior walls to improve the acoustics. Outside the courtyard stands the Venetian bell-tower built in 1682.

Just above the village are the remains of an earlier fortified settlement. Its houses are built one next to the other, for better protection from pirates. There are also the ruins of a prison dating from the time

The rock of Araklis, outside the village of Anogi

of the English occupation.

The road out of the village is rather unusual. Two massive rocks, like statues carved by some giant, stand like vigilant guards. The locals call them Araklis (or Heracles, 8 m in height) and the Rider.

After another 5 km., you arrive in **Stavros**, the main village of northern Ithaki, built in the foothills of Mt. Niritos. Stavros was founded by inhabitants of Anogi and Exogi in the 16th century. At that time it was a populous town, where the merchants from the surrounding villages met, and a way station between the ports of Polis and Frikes. Today its population has trickled away to a mere 250, but it remains an important crossroads.

In the village square stands the Byzantine temple of the Saviour. If you happen to be in Stavros on August 5 or 6, you can take part in the island's biggest festival, held at this church. The only bust of Odysseus on the island stands in the

The island's only bust of the hero Odysseus in the square in Stavros

The Tzouganatos home, one of Stavros' traditional buildings

park in the square. The Tzouganatos home, built in the 16th century as a headquarters for the island's governor, is one of Stavros' most traditional buildings. As far as accommodations and amenities are concerned, there are three hotels and plenty of rooms to rent, plus tourist shops and tavernas. In the Pilikata Archaeological Museum in Stavros (on Aredatidos Street, open daily excepting Monday) finds are exhibited from Loizos Cave, Pilikata and the School of Homer.

A downhill road takes you one km further on to the small blue-green harbour of Polis, where the island's fishing-boats are moored. You can relax and enjoy a cup of coffee or other drink in the area's only coffee bar. And you, adorers of diving, prepare! On the sea bottom an old town has been lying since the earthquake of 967 AD submerged it. It may be the Jerusalem mentioned in Anna Comnene's "Alexia" of 1089. When describing the circumstances of Guiscard's death, she mentions the town of Jerusalem standing opposite Fiskardo; it had been prophesied that Guiscard would die there. In the Roussanos area, where the town may have stood, tombs dating from the Christian era were discovered. To the right of the town of Polis lies the **Cave of Loizos**. It was a centre of worship for the island's early Helladic civilisation until the 1st century AD. Some believe this to be the

Cave of the Nymphs, even though the artefacts found in it date from a much earlier time. The cave was looted at the beginning of the 19th century, but the antiquities-hunters were unlucky. In later excavations carried out by Vollgraff, prehistoric vessels with incised letters were discovered, along with amphoras (the amphoras in which Odysseus carried Alcinous' gifts?), twelve bronze tripods dating from 800-700 BC, figurines of nymphs and other offerings. One of the most important finds is a piece of a woman's clay mask from 300-200 BC, bearing the inscription "EYXHN O¢Y-™ ™EI" (dedicated to Odysseus) which testifies to subsequent worship of the hero. All these finds are on exhibit in the museum in Stavros.

Between Stavros and Platrithias is **Pilikata** hill or the hill of Hermes; some experts believe Odysseus' palace was located here. Here, too, Homer's reference to three seas and three mountains holds true, corroborating their opinion. Excavations in 1929-1939 by British archaeologists brought to light remains of settlements dating from Neolithic times (2700 BC) up to the Classical era. This continuous habitation was perhaps due to the fertility of the soil. Of special interest are the two shards bearing inscriptions in the script known as Linear A. They were interpreted by Professor Paul Fore of the University of Indiana as reading: "THE NYMPH SAVED ME" and "HERE IS WHAT I, AREDATIS, GIVE TO ANASSA THE GODDESS RHEA: 100 GOATS, 10 SHEEP, 3 PIGS". A rock tomb and an altar were discovered in the ancient cemetery.

You leave Stavros and drive up to the Homeric mountain Neion, now known as **Exogi** (outside the world). It was given this name from the fact that it is the northernmost and most isolated village in

Pilikata Hill, the town's harbour and Loizos cave. This historic region was continuously inhabited from the Neolithic era until Byzantine times

The village of Exogi clinging to Homer's Neion. The Monastery of the Panagia Eleoussa can be seen. Further down are the 1933 pyramids and the Church of Agia Marina

Ithaki. It was settled in medieval times, when it was known as Stavronikion and was the island's third-largest town. Built at an elevation of 340 m, it was well protected from pirate invasions and was also a good spot from which to observe the sea all around. After piracy was wiped out, the town's peasant population dwindled away here, too. Out of a population of 500 at the turn of the century, only 20 inhabitants remain today. The village is surrounded by vast man-made terraces planted with grapevines and cypress-trees. The few rooms to rent in the tiny houses clinging to the green hillside offer a breathtaking view of the coast, as well as a restful hermitage, far from the bustle of the more densely populated areas of the island. The silence may be broken temporarily by the crowds of visitors that descend on the village each July 17 to attend the festival at the 19th-century Church of Agia Marina.

The old Monastery of the Panagia Eleoussa

Continuing on up the mountain, you come to three pyramids, built in 1933. The first is the tomb of the mother of their builder, C. Papadopoulos, the second has an inscription and a built-in jug containing coins from various countries, and the third is the tomb of Papadopoulos himself. After another two km, you arrive at the Pernarakia locale, on the hill's highest peak. It is the site of the monastery of Panagia Eleoussa, which has not been in use since World War II, except on the Tuesday after Easter. From this vantage-point, one has an unham-

The village of Platrithia, as built after the pirates were wiped out in the 16th century. The Church of the Taxiarhi can be seen on the hill of the same name

pered view of all the Ionian islands and beyond to the coast of northern Greece, and sometimes even to the coast of Italy.

Built in one of the more fertile areas of the island is **Platrithias**. The name is a composite of two words, "plati" and "rithron", which mean wide furrow. Contributing factors to the village's continuous habitation from antiquity up to and including the early Christian era were the fertile soil, abundant water and ease of communication with nearby ports. This situation held until the pirates made their appearance and the villagers sought refuge in more mountainous areas. They returned after the 16th century and created a town of 1000 inhabitants; today the population has been reduced to 400. The villagers work at farming, stock breeding and fishing. On Taxiarhi hill stands the Church of the Taxiarhi built around the 11th century; up to the late 19th century it was used as a monastery. It took on its present appearance after the 1953 earthquakes. The Church of the Panagia in Melanidro, between Platrithias and Exogi, holds a celebration every year on August 15 in the square. Everyone is automatically invited by the hospitable villagers. Platrithias is the administrative centre for the hamlets of Messovouno, Kolieri, Lahos, Agii Saranda and Limnes.

Above Platrithias in the direction of Mt. Exogi is another Homeric locality, Melanydrus spring (called Melanithros by

Ruins of buildings in the "School of Homer"

the locals) which has therapeutic properties. It took its name from the dark ("melanos") colour of its mud. It is said to have provided water for the area around the School of Homer and that Homer, who was blind up to that time, regained his sight from its therapeutic waters. A little farther down is a well, to which you will descend by some stairs. The locals call it "Penelope's Baths". In reality, it is a Mycenean vaulted tomb. The now ruined Church of Agios Athanassios (600 AD) was built using ancient masonry.

In the area known as the School of Homer near the Church of Agios Athanassios, short-lived excavations in 1905 by Goekoop and Vollgraff brought to light ruins of buildings of a significant settlement and looted tombs from historical times. Here, too, suspicions were aroused as to whether this was Odysseus' town. Artefacts from the 4th century AD testify to the presence of Romans in the area.

From the town square in Platrithias a paved road brings us after one km to

The stone pyramid in the outdoor folklore "museum" in Kolieri square

Kolieri, built on the western side of Afales Bay. A landmark here is the folk-art monument as you enter the village, a pyramid of millstones and an old olive press, the work of E. Raftopoulos after 1953. On the same road you will come to the now abandoned hamlet of **Kalamos**. The Springs of Kalamos, as the name suggests, is an area with plenty of spring-water and abundant greenery. This is the site of the island's one source of water, which at one time fed six springs. The

Afales Gulf is the island's biggest

A traditional two-story house which was used as a hotel until the 1953 earthquakes

One of the traditional Neoclassical homes in the Lahos area

Tikti Spring of Kalamos, or as certain experts have called it, Coracopetra, starts from the well and winds up at Arethusa. Today this spring provides water for the plain that extends as far as Afales. The traditional two-story building with the battlements was a hotel until 1953. West of the Bay is another ruined village, Ai-Lias.

From the square in Platrithia an unpaved road begins which leads us down to the sandy beach on the biggest bay in Ithaki, Afales. There you can swim, fish, or take a hike up to Mt. Marmakas, on the island's northernmost cape of the same name. East of the mountain is Cape Krokali, Homer's Crocyleia. On May 21, 1941, the Greek battleship "Papanikolis" torpedoed five German ships here.

On the road from Platrithias to Frikes, you will encounter Agii Saranda and Lahos. This area escaped extensive damages in the catastrophic earthquakes, so

The picturesque little harbour and the jetty in Frikes are graced by mills

you will see traditional houses with Venetian and Neoclassical elements still standing. In the abandoned farming district of Marmakas there is a well-preserved mill.

Frikes is a tiny fishing village, built in a fertile valley between Mts. Niritos and Marmakas. The village's houses are scattered here and there in the valley, where as recently as the past century pirates took refuge and organised their raids. It is even believed that the village took its name either from a pirate or from the ancient god Phorcys. It has been inhabited since the 16th century. Below the village lie a lovely bay and a picturesque jetty with mills; here caiques and fishing-boats are moored. Some archaeologists believe this to be Homer's port of Reithron, used for commercial transactions and as a fishing ground. On a rock to the right the firing of the Nazi ship "Antoinetta" by Greek freedom fighters on September 13, 1944 is commemorated.

Blue-green water off the small beach of Limenia

The village's 100 permanent residents continue to be occupied in fishing, farming and the tourist industry: the area attracts quite a few visitors every summer, as it is an ideal vacation spot for lovers of the sea and fishing. The village offers both hotels and rooms to rent. Along the harbour are cafeterias and tavernas, where one can enjoy a meal in the open air beside the sea. So don't forget to taste the fish – the previous night's

The tavernas in the little port are full of people enjoying a meal of fresh fish

A ruined mill in the quaint "stone" village of Rahi

catch is brought fresh to the island every morning. The handicraft workshop "Elpinor" also serves as an exhibition centre. Outside Frikes are Limenia and Kourvoulia beaches.

After the small inlet known as Plakoutses, the road from Frikes passes some ruined mills and after 4 km arrives in **Rahi**. This is a tiny hamlet clinging to the side of a hill. Its small houses are beautifully built of stone in the old traditional way. At the top of the hill, with superb scenery spread out at its feet, stands the Church of Panagia Evangelistria, which houses a fine altar-screen. A little further on, on the historic Bay of Mavronas, the area's inhabitants fought the pirates in 1650 and defeated them. The ruined monastery of Ai-Nikola was in use until the earthquake in 1953. Inside its church, the altar is supported by an ancient column capital, possibly from some ancient temple in the area or from a shipwreck.

The traditional town of Kioni, the loveliest on the island, brings to mind a famous painting

The three partly demolished mills at the Psigadi locale at the entrance to the gulf

There are also some ruins of the English customs house, which was demolished in 1967.

The road runs downhill to **Kioni**. This traditional island village spreads like an amphitheatre down from Rahi towards the sea until it halts before an enclosed, spacious little harbour, where the luxury yachts of foreign visitors are moored. The village most likely took its name from a piece of an ancient column ("kioni") used as a pedestal for the altar in some church. Kioni was another hiding-place and base of operations for pirates and no islanders lived there before the early 16th century. In 1800 it had 1000 inhabitants, who worked chiefly as tillers of the soil and fishermen. Ships from other parts of the island came and went in its busy harbour and trade flourished. After 1900 its population gradually began to dwindle; now tourism has been added to the occupations of its remaining 200 inhabitants.

The house where the hero of the Greek War of Independence Karaiskakis lived until 1821

Still standing on the harbour's right-hand side is part of the stone house where the hero of the Greek War of Independence George Karaiskakis lived before 1821. At the Psigadi locale stand three partly demolished mills, which until World War I ground flour for the villagers and the inhabitants of the surrounding area; today they grace the entrance to the bay. In Kioni you will find accommodations in hotels and rooms to rent, and meals and refreshments in the village's tavernas and small coffee-shops.

Built on the rocks of Cape Profitis Ilias is the small chapel of the same name. Every year on July 20, the villagers go to mass in boats. In the evening a festival is held in honour of the Saint. The 18th-century Church of Agios Ioannis holds its saint's-day celebrations on June 24. Visitors can hire a boat in the village's harbour to take them to the nearby beaches

A large part of the region's picturesqueness is due to the simplicity of life

The small village of Lefki, built on the green slope of Mt. Niritos

of Katsikouli, Sarakinari, Plakoutses and Filiatro. Fishing enthusiasts should get a good supply of bait and get ready to catch some big ones! Caiques sail to the more distant beaches at Nidri, Lefkada and Skorpios.

On the way back, you will pass through Stavros again. **Lefki**, 14 km before Vathi, is built on the steep western side of Mt. Niritos. Its charming little houses nestled in greenery were built with British aid after the earthquake. Former residents of the village were pirates who exploited its position to plunder passing ships. The islanders in turn used the situation of the village to their advantage in helping freedom fighters during the Italian and German occupations. In the Church of the Presentation of the Virgin is a carved wooden altar-screen brought there late in the 19th century by Greeks who had emigrated to Odessa or

Sun and sea – your inseparable companions on your journey to the Ionian Islands

The windmill towering above the small beach of Aspros Gialos

Trieste. A few rooms to rent are available in the village, and meals may be had in neighbouring Stavros. You can swim at the sand beaches of Megaloni, Kaminia and Amoudaki. There are also a few rooms to rent and a small taverna on the beach. After a swim in the crystal-clear water, you can quench your thirst at one of the wells in the area. On the site of the Ai-Giorgis chapel there was a monastery before the Venetian occupation. The monks came to a sorry end when Mohammedan pirates attacked and killed them. Near Mirtera beach is Fokotripa cave. From Lefki, it is 3 km down to Aspros Gialos, one of Ithaki's finest beaches. The last village on our itinerary is **Ai-Giannis**. The tiny houses of this small village seem to be pinned to the lush green hill. This quiet, superb beach and the rocky shores ideal for fishing will hopefully convince you to stay a little longer than you had planned.

How to Get There

You can reach Kefalonia on the ferries sailing from:
Patra in the Peloponnese via Sami in Kefalonia via Pisso Aetos in Ithaki to Fiskardo in Kefalonia,
Killini in the Peloponnese to Poros in Kefalonia,
Killini in the Peloponnese to Argostoli in Kefalonia.

Flying dolphins link Patra in the Peloponnese to Argostoli in Kefalonia.

Kefalonia is linked to the rest of the Ionian islands and to mainland Greece by ferry-boat:
from Skinari in Zakinthos to Pessada in Kefalonia,
from Vassiliki in Lefkada to Fiskardo in Kefalonia,
from Nidri in Lefkada via Fiskardo in Kefalonia to Frikes in Ithaki,
from Agia Efimia in Kefalonia to Vathi in Ithaki,
from Agia Efimia in Kefalonia to Astakos in Epirus.

You can get to Patra and Killini on an inter-city bus (KTEL Kefalinias) whose terminus is in Kifissos Street in Athens, or by train from the Stathmos Peloponnese also in Athens.

Olympic Airways flies between its airport in Athens and Sarlata, near Argostoli in Kefalonia.

Useful Phone Numbers

Argostoli:	Argostoli Municipality	0671-	22230,22240
	Greek National Tourist Organisation Offices		22248
	Police		22200
	Harbour Master's Office		22224, 22202
	Hospital		22434, 24641
	Children's Hospital		28550
	Olympic Airways		41511, 28808, 28881
	Archaeological Museum		28300
	Historical Archives		23451
	Korgialenio Historical and Folklore Museum		28835
Lixouri:	Town Hall	0671-	91326, 91208
	KTEL Inter-city Buses		92733
	Police		91207, 91909
	Harbour Master's Office		91205
	Hospital		91233, 92222, 91194
	Petritsios Library		91222
	Public Library-Tipaldon Iakovaton Museum		91325

List of Hotels

BUHAYER, P.**	Argostoli	A	0671-	22766
FOKAS, D.**	Argostoli	A		23511
GALIATSATOU, E.**	Argostoli	A		23126
GNESSOULIS, A.**	Argostoli	A		25331
HARITOS, P.**	Argostoli	A		24576
HUGGENSTEIN, H.**	Argostoli	A		24311
KALOGIRATOS, D.**	Argostoli	A		24939
KAOUKI, E.**	Argostoli	A		23037
KARAVA, E.**	Argostoli	A		28710
KARAVIOTIS, P.**	Argostoli	A		28297
KOUTAVAS, N. **	Argostoli	A		22171
KROUSSOS, P.**	Argostoli	A		23398
LEONIDAKIS, Z.**	Argostoli	A		22081

LINARDATOS, G.**	Argostoli	A	28415
LOUKATOS, G.**	Argostoli	A	24302
MALIAGROU, A.**	Argostoli	A	28345
MARKETOS, E.**	Argostoli	A	28460
METALINOS, I.**	Argostoli	A	22383
MONETSANTOU, M.**	Argostoli	A	24363
MONOKROUSSOS, G.**	Argostoli	A	24312
MOSHONA, D.**	Argostoli	A	23121
MOSHONAS, E.**	Argostoli	A	23483
PAPADATOS, S.**	Argostoli	A	23242
SARLOU, D.**	Argostoli	A	28238
SKLAVOUNAKIS, N.**	Argostoli	A	23396
STELLATOS, G.**	Argostoli	A	28286
TZIVRAS, G.**	Argostoli	A	22628
TZOUGANATOU, G.**	Argostoli	A	22411
VARTELATOS, N.**	Argostoli	A	24038
ZERVOU, A.**	Argostoli	A	28919
ALEXANDRATOS, P.**	Argostoli	B	22129
PAVLATOS, G.**	Argostoli	B	28964
ROUHOTA, V.**	Argostoli	B	28017
VARTELATOS, S.**	Argostoli	B	24285
AENOS*	Argostoli	C	28013
BYRON*	Argostoli	C	23401
CASTELLO*	Argostoli	C	23520
FOKAS*	Argostoli	C	28100
GALAXY*	Argostoli	C	24096
IONIAN PLAZA*	Argostoli	C	25581-4
KEFALONIAN STAR*	Argostoli	C	23180
MIRABEL*	Argostoli	C	25381
MUIKIS*	Argostoli	C	23032
OLGA*	Argostoli	C	24981
REGINA*	Argostoli	C	23557
TOURIST*	Argostoli	C	22510
ALEGRO*	Argostoli	D	22268
CHARA*	Argostoli	D	22427
EUROPE APARTMENTS*	Argostoli		22088
MIRA-MARE*	Argostoli		25511

ANTONATOS, P.**	Lassi	A	0671- 28764
AVGOUSTATOU, I.**	Lassi	A	22177
GALIATSATOS, G.**	Lassi	A	23433
GALIATSOU, M.**	Lassi	A	31085
KALAFATIS, I.**	Lassi	A	23767
KALAFATIS, N.**	Lassi	A	24334
KATSETI, D.**	Lassi	A	28708
LEONIDAKIS, N.**	Lassi	A	28231
MARKATOS, K.**	Lassi	A	22881
MEDITERRANEE*	Lassi	A	28760-3
MELA, M.**	Lassi	A	23036
PARTHENIS, G.**	Lassi	A	28210
STEFANATOS, M.**	Lassi	A	23551
TRAVLOS, M.**	Lassi	A	23486
TZIVRAS, G.**	Lassi	A	22628
VIKATOS, P.**	Lassi	A	24547
VLAHOU, V.**	Lassi	A	28336
ANTONATOS, A.**	Lassi	B	28764
FOKAS, I.**	Lassi	B	28016
LEONIDAKIS, Z.**	Lassi	B	22169

MOUSSIKIS, N.**	Lassi	B		23460
TSOUTOUFLI, E.**	Lassi	B		22284
VIKATOS, P.**	Lassi	B		25742
VLAHOS, D.**	Lassi	B		22234
VLAHOS, S.**	Lassi	B		24550
IRILENA*	Lassi	C		23118
LASSI*	Lassi	C		23126
LORENZO*	Lassi	C		28783
PRINCESS*	Lassi			25501
WHITE ROCKS*	Platis Gialos	A	0671-	28332
DIMITRATOS, G.**	Lourdata	A	0671-	31221
GALIATSATOS, A.**	Lourdata	A		31082
HARALAMBATOS, H.**	Lourdata	A		31276
KANTZOU, M.**	Lourdata	A		31150
PETROUTSOS, N.**	Lourdata	A		31221
KAMILATOS, A.**	Lourdata	C		31206
BOUZOU, A.**	Peratata	A	0671-	22251
FRANGISKATOS, H.**	Peratata	A		69086
STAMATATOS, A.**	Peratata	A		69342
STAMATATOS, G.**	Peratata	A		69496
MARKATOS, P.**	Peratata	B		69305
PAPADATOS, P.**	Peratata	B		69547
PAPADATOU, E.**	Peratata	C		69493
PODARA, S.**	Razata	B	0671-	24321
FILIPATOS, S.**	Kourkoumelata	A	0671-	41384
KANAKI, K.**	Kourkoumelata	B		41385
FRANGIAS, S.**	Svoronata	A	0671-	41861
KOUNADI, S.**	Svoronata	A		41306
TETENES, I.**	Svoronata	A		41383
MOSHOPOULOS, N.**	Domata	A	0671-	41652
BOURA, A.**	Spartia	A	0671-	23505
DRAKOPOULOS, S.**	Spartia	A		69008
LIOSSATOS, A.**	Spartia	A		69136
MESSOLORAS, H.**	Spartia	A		69244
MORAITIS, D.**	Spartia	A		69521
RESIDENCE POSEIDON**	Spartia	A		69649
STELATOS, S.**	Spartia	A		89293
LIOSSATOS, A.**	Spartia	B		69251
ZOUMBOULIS, E.**	Spartia	B		69113
SKOUTELAS, I.**	Karavados	A	0671-	23047
ISMAILOS, G.**	Minies	A	0671-	22842
MARKATOU, A.**	Minies	A		22720
MOULINOS, G.**	Minies	A		23764
PETRATOS, S.**	Minies	A		41500
VAGELATOS, K.**	Minies	A		23862
MARAVAGIAS, F.**	Lakithra	A	0671-	41204
MOUIKI, A.**	Lakithra	A		91691

MOUIKI, E.**	Lakithra	A		41562
ATSAROU, A.**	Lixouri	A	0671-	91911
DRAKOPOULOU, A.**	Lixouri	A		92442
KEFALLONIA PALACE*	Lixouri	A		91111
KOKINIS, G.**	Lixouri	A		91593
SIMONETOU, Z.**	Lixouri	A		91425
TOUMASSIS, N.**	Lixouri	A		91148
VARSAKI, M.**	Lixouri	A		91938
IL GIARDINO*	Lixouri	B		92505
TERRA MARE*	Lixouri	B		92361
PALATINO*	Lixouri	C		92700
POSSIDON*	Lixouri	C		92518
SUMMERY*	Lixouri	C		91771
VASSALAS, P.**	Kouvalata	A	0671-	91455
LAZARATOS, A.**	Kouvalata	B		91500
LOUKERIS, E.**	Lepeda	A	0671-	91971
MOURELATOS, G.**	Lepeda	A		21691
APERGIS, D.**	Zola	A	0671-	85278
APERGIS, G.**	Zola	A		85276
HARALAMBATOS, A.**	Vlahata	A	0671-	31252
MIHALATOS, G.**	Vlahata	A		31217
TZIVRAS, I.**	Vlahata	A		28703
HARALAMBATOS, M.**	Vlahata	B		31291
BALTSAVIAS, S.**	Dilinata	B	0671-	84050
TZORTZATOU, E.**	Dilinata	B		84073
FOKA, K.**	Spilia	B	0671-	28727
FERDERIGOS, N.**	Katelios	A	0671-	81274
FOTINATOS, S.**	Katelios	A		81371
KOURKOUMELIS, D.**	Katelios	A		81363
MANENDIS, D.**	Katelios	A		81122
MARKETOS, D.**	Katelios	A		81084
PANTELIOU, E.**	Katelios	A		81353
PAPADATOS, G.**	Katelios	A		81372
PAPADATOS, N.**	Katelios	A		81356
THEOHARITSIS, A.**	Katelios	A		81161
TSILIMIDAS, A.**	Markopoulo	A	0674-	81333
FAMBIATOU, S.**	Skala	A	0674-	28564
GROUZIS, D.**	Skala	A		83231
HATZIDAKI, L.**	Skala	A		83358
KOURIS, A.**	Skala	A		83207
KOURKOUMELIS, G.**	Skala	A		83224
METAXA, M.**	Skala	A		23246
SOLOMOS, S.**	Skala	A		93879
SPATHIS, A.**	Skala	A		83264
TRAVLOS, P.**	Skala	A		83398
TSIMARAS, A.**	Skala	A		83394
ZAPANTIS, D.**	Skala	A		83283
ZAPANTIS, G.**	Skala	A		83260

ZAPANTIS, M.**	Skala	A		83322
ANINOS, D.**	Skala	B		83345
KORKOS A.**	Skala	B		83233
KOURKOUMELI, S.**	Skala	B		83312
KOURKOUMELIS, N.**	Skala	B		83230
TRAVLOS, P.**	Skala	B		83208
ZAPANTIS, F.**	Skala	B		83319
ZAPANTIS, N.**	Skala	B		22965
MIHALITSIANOU, A.**	Ratzakli	A	0674-	28339
PANTELIOS, D.**	Ratzakli	A		41777
ZAPANTI, E.**	Hionata	A	0674-	83226
ANTONATOS, D.**	Sami	A	0674-	22301
GIAKOUMATOU, S.**	Sami	A		22706
STRINTZI, E.**	Sami	A		22520
VASSILATOU, N.**	Sami	A		22374
VINIERATOU, A.**	Sami	A		22542
VANGELATOS, N.**	Sami	G		22485
GOUNTINAKI, A.**	Sami	B		22321
KOUNADI, H.**	Sami	B		22246
PANTELATOS, M.**	Sami	B		22076
PERICLES*	Sami	B		22780
RASSIA, T.**	Sami	B		22711
SAMI BEACH*	Sami	B		22824
CASTLE OF SAMI*	Sami	C		22656
MANOLATOU, V.**	Sami	C		22058
MELISSANI*	Sami	D		22464
KRINOS*	Sami	E		32002
TOULATOS, P.**	Poulata	A	0674-	—
PAVOURIS, S.**	Divarata	A	0674-	61137
KAVALIERATOS, G.**	Karavomilos	A	0674-	61237
TZORTZATOS, A.**	Karavomilos	C		22226
KOLAITIS, S.**	Poros	A	0674-	72521
KOUSTOUMBARDIS, N.**	Poros	A		72445
KRITIKOS, G.**	Poros	A		72471
METAXAS, P.**	Poros	A		72492
MIHALITSIANOS, A.**	Poros	A		72492
MILIARESSIS, D.**	Poros	A		72407
MILIARESSIS, H.**	Poros	A		72011
MILIARESSIS, P.**	Poros	A		72041
PAPADOGIANNAKI, H.**	Poros	A		72484
PAVLIDOU, M.**	Poros	A		72314
PETRATOS, G.**	Poros	A		72336
RAFTOPOULOS, D.**	Poros	A		72028
RAFTOPOULOS, D.**	Poros	A		72314
ROMANOS, G.	Poros	A		72280
SIMOTAS, A.**	Poros	A		72204
SIMOTAS, E.**	Poros	A		72310
STELATOU, D.**	Poros	A		72487
TZAMARIAS, F.**	Poros	A		72428
TZAMARIAS, G.**	Poros	A		72445
TZAMARIAS, I.**	Poros	A		73216

VAVASSIS, D.**	Poros	A		72495
BELVEDERE (APARTMENTS)*	Poros	B		72493
HERCULES*	Poros	B		72351
KOUTROKOIS, G.**	Poros	B		72300
CEFALOS*	Poros	C		72139
LUISA APARTMENTS*	Poros	C		72572
GALINI*	Poros	E		72353
ALEXATOU, M.**	Agia Efimia	A	0674-	61256
AMITSIS, S.**	Agia Efimia	A		61105
BALAS, E.**	Agia Efimia	A		61039
DENDRINOS, S.**	Agia Efimia	A		61392
KOYTSOGIORGOU, V.**	Agia Efimia	A		61237
MAKRI, S.**	Agia Efimia	A		61338
PAPADATOS, G.**	Agia Efimia	A		61367
RAFTOPOULOS, P.**	Agia Efimia	A		61233
STAMOULIS, P.**	Agia Efimia	A		61336
SKIADARESSIS, D.**	Agia Efimia	B		61319
VRETOS, A.**	Agia Efimia	B		31629
ZAFIRATOU, F.**	Agia Efimia	B		61238
LOGARA APARTMENTS*	Agia Efimia	C		61202
MOUSTAKIS*	Agia Efimia	C		61030
PYLAROS*	Agia Efimia	C		61210
VRETOS, G.**	Agia Efimia	C		61090
KOKOLI, E.**	Assos	A	0674-	51526
LINARDOS, L.**	Assos	A		51563
PAPASPIRATOS, S.**	Assos	A		51360
SKIADARESSI, E.**	Assos	A		51360
SKIADARESSI, V.**	Assos	A		51376
STEFANATOS, V.**	Assos	A		51358
PAPADAKOS, P.**	Assos	B		51381
ROKKOS, A.**	Assos	B		51523
VAROTSIS, V.**	Assos	B		61524
THEODORATOU, A.**	Assos	C		51530
BARZOUKAS, D.**	Fiskardo	A	0674-	51478
KOULOUMBARISTI, A.**	Fiskardo	A		51346
KOUNAVI, A.**	Fiskardo	A		51573
PALIKISSIANOU, V.**	Fiskardo	A		51471
SOUPIONA, O.**	Fiskardo	A		51496
TZAMARELOS, I.**	Fiskardo	A		51484
KAVADIAS, G.**	Fiskardo	B		51487
KONIDARI, D.**	Fiskardo	B		51569
PATRIKIOS, N.**	Fiskardo	B		51432
TSELENTI, E.**	Fiskardo	B		32633
TSELENTI, S.**	Fiskardo	B		51342
AERI, A.**	Manganos	A	0674-	51603
PATRIKIOS, N.**	Manganos	A		51432
GIANNOULATOS, G.**	Manganos	B		51593
GIANNOPOULOS, I.**	Tzamarelata	A	0674-	51612
FERENTINOS, S.**	Enossi	A	0674-	51230
DENDRINOS, P.**	Antipata	A	0674-	51493
KOKOLIS, P.**	Antipata	B		51542

THOMAKOU, A.**	Antipata	B		51427
VRIONIS, I.**	Kothreas	A	0674-	51511
KAKIAS, P.**	Kothreas	B		—
KONIDARIS, G.**	Matsoukata	B	0674-	51282
DELAPORTAS, G.**	Ithaki	A	0674-	32104
KARAVIAS, E.**	Ithaki	A		32267
KOSTIRI, H.**	Ithaki	A		33180
KOSTOPOULOS, O.**	Ithaki	A		33130
KOULOURI, A.**	Ithaki	A		32387
LAZARIS, E.**	Ithaki	A		32587
LIVANIS, E.**	Ithaki	A		33080
MAVROKEFALOS, G.**	Ithaki	A		31473
MORFESSIS, G.**	Ithaki	A		33138
PAXINOU, M.**	Ithaki	A		31785
RAFTOPOULOS, P.**	Ithaki	A		31733
SIMIRIS, S.**	Ithaki	A		32717
SOMBOLAS, A.**	Ithaki	A		31245
VLASSOPOULOS, T.**	Ithaki	A		32322
XANTHOPOULOS, K.**	Ithaki	A		32587
ANAGNOSTATOU, V.**	Ithaki	B		51144
DELAPORTA, M.**	Ithaki	B		32128
HANOS, E.**	Ithaki	B		32448
KARATZIS, T.**	Ithaki	B		31679
KOSTOPOULOS, O.**	Ithaki	B		33130
KOUTSOUVELIS, D.**	Ithaki	B		31692
LAZARIS, E.**	Ithaki	B		32239
MAROUDAS, D.**	Ithaki	B		32751
RAFTOPOULOS, P.**	Ithaki	B		31735
SERVOU, P.**	Ithaki	B		32055
SIMIRIS, A.**	Ithaki	B		33136
KALINIKOS, A.**	Ithaki	C		31580
VLASSOPOULOU, V.**	Ithaki	C		32119

*Hotel
**Rooms to Rent

Bibliography

ANAGNOSTATOS, ANDREAS L.: "Historical and Folkloric Miscellany of Ithaki", Spiros Dendrinos Publications, 1993.
BENETATOS, IOULIANOS: "Far(i)ssa and the Farissians, Tradition-Folklore-Customs", Athens, 1990.
DEMBONOS, ANGELOS-DIONISSIS: "Argostoli Amuses Itself", Argostoli, 1979.
DEMBONOS, ANGELOS-DIONISSIS: "Magical Medicine in Kefalonia", Argostoli, 1983.
DEMBONOS, ANGELOS-DIONISSIS: "The Philharmonic School of Kefalonia 1838-1940", a publication of the Kefalonia Nomarchy's Committee for Popular Education, Argostoli, 1988.
DEMBONOS, ANGELOS-DIONISSIS: "The Years of the Italian and German Occupation and the National Resistance in Kefalonia and Ithaki", Vol. I "The Fascist Italian Occupation, the National Liberation Organisations and their Resistance Achievements in Kefalonia and Ithaki", ODEB, Athens, 1987.
DENDRINOS, SPIROS: "Fiskardo Then and Now", Spiros Dendrinos publications.
DESTOUNIS, GEORGIOS: "Kefaliniaka", Athens, 1968.
FOKAS-KOSMETATOS, NIKOLAOS: "The Castle of Agios Georgios in Kefalonia, The Old Capital of the Island", Athens, 1966.
FRANGOPOULOS, I. & MALERAKI, I.: "A Hydrogeological and Geochemical Study of the Island of Kefalonia", Bulletin of Scientific Research, No. 1 (YD), Athens, 1963.

GALIATSATOU, BETA S.: "During the Hours of the Earthquakes in Kefalonia", Athens, 1959.
GELIS, KONSTANTINOS G., Arch-Presbyter: "Agios Gerassimos of Kefalinia", Second Edition, Holy Monastery of Agios Gerassimos, Athens, 1978.
GELIS, KONSTANTINOS G., Arch-Presbyter: "The Holy Monastery of Agia Paraskevi Lepedon and Saint Anthimos Kourouklis", Athens, 1973.
KALINIKOS, A.. DENDRINOS, S.: "Ithaki Then and Now", Spiros Dendrinos Publications.
KOLETAS, S.C.: "Ancient Mythology of Kefalonia and Ithaki", 1977.
KONDOGIANATOS, B: "Lixouriotika", Vol. II "From Religion, the People and Life", Koridalos, 1980.
KONSTANDAKATOS, E.T.: "The Rock that Moves", Argostoli, 1901.
KOSMETATOS, E.: "Report on the Roads of Kefalonia", Korgialenio Historical and Folklore Museum, 1991.
LIVIERATOS, EFSTATHIOS K.: "History of the Island of Kefalonia", Piraeus 1988.
LOUKATOS, GERASSIMOS S.: "Images and Memories from Old Kefalonia, Experiences, Testimonies", Filipotis Publications, Athens, 1991.
LOUKATOS, SPIROS D.: "The Years of the Italian and German Occupation and the National Resistance in Kefalonia and Ithaki", Vol. II, "The Italian-German Conflict in Kefalonia and the Contribution of the National Liberation Organisations to the Demonstration of 8-24 September 1943", Addendum, "The Conflict on the Other Ionian Islands", a publication of the Brotherhood of Kefalonians and Ithacans of Piraeus, Athens, 1981.
LOUKATOS, SPIROS D.: "The Years of the Italian and German Occupation and the National Resistance in Kefalonia and Ithaki", Vol. III, "The Nazi German Occupation, the National Liberation Organisations and their Resistance Achievements in Kefalonia and Ithaki, 24 September 1943-17 September 1944", a publication of the Federation of Kefalonian and Ithacan Societies and the Faraklata Association "I Evgiros", Athens, 1991.
MARINATOS, S. N.: "Kefalonia, a Historical and Archaeological Walk", T.E.T. of Kefalonia publications, 1962.
MATTHEOS, SOCRATES: "Kefalinia IV, a Better Future", Athens, 1978.
MAVROMIHALI, REBECCA S.: "Kithnos and Kefalonia, My Blue Journeys", Dodoni Publications, Athens-Giannina, 1988.
MOSHOPOULOS, EVANGELOS: "History of Kefalonia, Kefalonia our Best Beloved", Second Edition, Revised and Enlarged, Athens 1982.
MOSHOPOULOS, GEORGIOS N.: "History of Kefalonia", Vol. I, "From Ancient Times up to 1797", Second Revised Edition, Kefalos Publications, Athens, 1990.
MOSHOPOULOS, GEORGIOS N.: "History of Kefalonia", Vol. II, "1797-1940", Kefalos Publications, Athens, 1988.
MOSHOPOULOS, GERASSIMOS C.: "(A Short) History of Kefalonia", Athens, 1951.
PAXIMADOPOULOU-STAVRINOU, MIRANDA: "The Uprisings in Kefalinia in the Years 1848 and 1849", Society for Kefalonian Historical Research, Athens 1980.
PUPILS OF THE 2ND LYCEUM OF ARGOSTOLI: "Post-earthquake Argostoli as a Modern City", Argostoli, 1990.
SOCIETY FOR KEFALONIAN HISTORICAL STUDIES: "Kefalonian Chronicles", Vol. II, Argostoli, 1977.
SOCIETY FOR KEFALONIAN HISTORICAL STUDIES: "Kefalonian Chronicles", Vol. III, 1978-79, Argostoli, 1979.
SOCIETY FOR KEFALONIAN HISTORICAL STUDIES: "Kefalonian Chronicles", Vol. IV, 1980-82, Argostoli, 1982.
SOCIETY FOR KEFALONIAN HISTORICAL STUDIES: "Kefalonian Chronicles", Vol. V, Argostoli, 1986.
SOCIETY FOR KEFALONIAN HISTORICAL STUDIES: "Minutes of the 5th International Pan-Ionian Conference", Vol. I "History up to 1809", Argostoli, 1989.
SOCIETY FOR KEFALONIAN HISTORICAL STUDIES: "Minutes of the 5th International Pan-Ionian Conference", Vol. III "A. Archaeology – Art, B. Legal – Developmental Topics", Argostoli, 1991.
TOUBIS, M.: "Kefalonia, History – Art – Folklore – Touring", Mihalis Toubis Publications, Athens, 1991.
TSITSELIS, ILIAS A.: "Kefalonian Miscellany", Vol. I, Athens, 1904.
TSITSELIS, ILIAS A.: "Kefalonian Miscellany", Vol. II, Athens, 1960.
TZOUGANATOS, NIKOLAOS: "Marinos Antipas and the Socialist Developments in Kefalonia", an Honorary Dedication to his Memory by the Brotherhood of Kefalonians and Ithacans of Piraeus, 1978.
VOUNAS, HRISTOS: "From the Piquant and Curious Folklore of Kefalonia", Journal "O Fanos tis Kefalonias", Argostoli, Patra, 1968.
"IOS", Illustrated Monthly Review, Director-Editor K. A. Papageorgiou, Athens, 1962.
"ZIZANION" Newspaper, Director and Editor Georgios Molfetas, Founded 1892.
Great Hellenic Encyclopaedia of Pavlos Drandakis, Vol. XXI, Phoenix Publishing House Ltd.

Index of Names

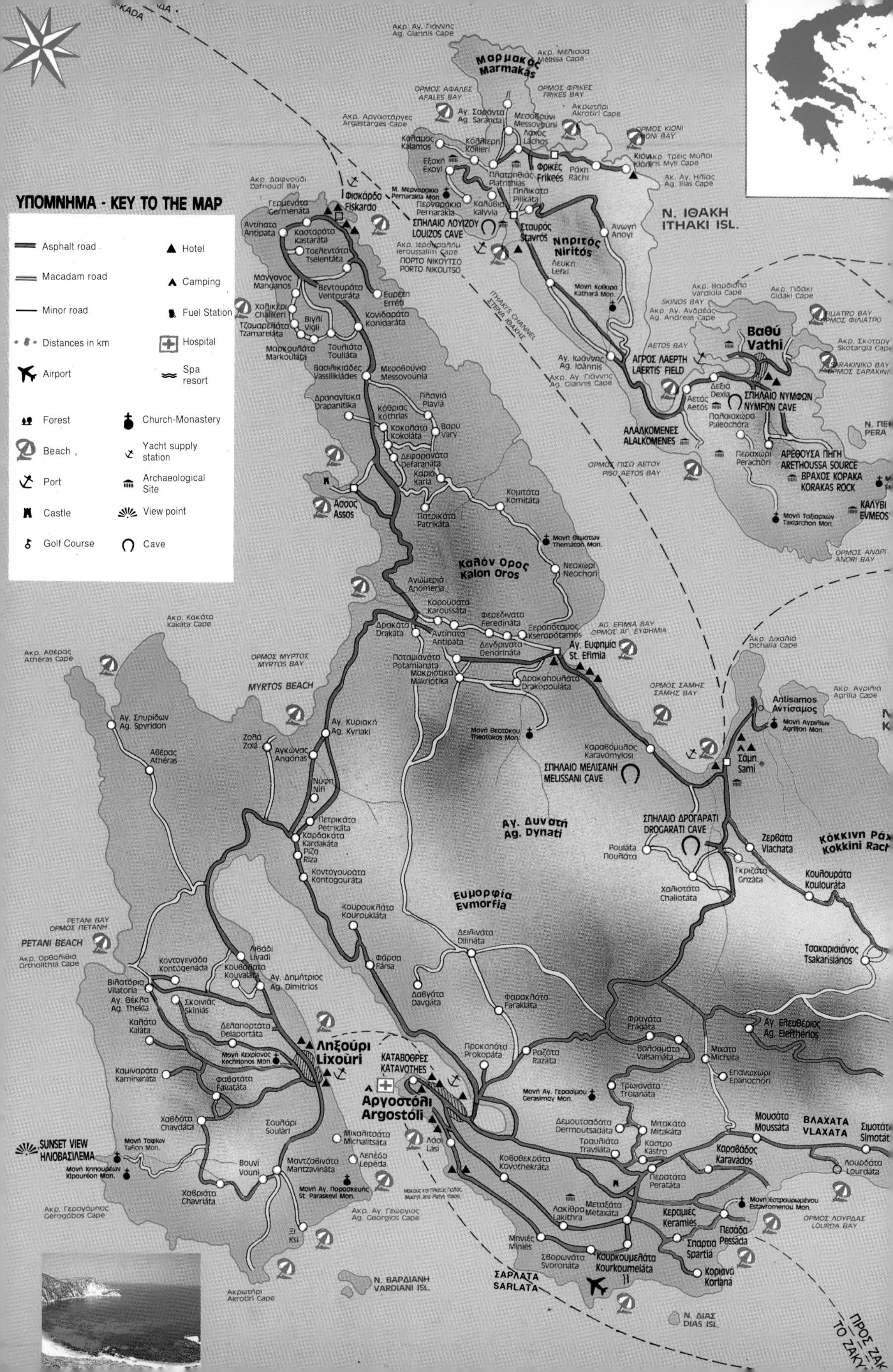

ΥΠΟΜΝΗΜΑ - KEY TO THE MAP
Asphalt road
Macadam road
Minor road
Distances in km
Airport
Forest
Beach
Port
Castle
Golf Course
Hotel
Camping
Fuel Station
Hospital
Spa resort
Church-Monastery
Yacht supply station
Archaeological Site
View point
Cave
Ν. ΙΘΑΚΗ
ITHAKI ISL.
Μαρμακάς
Marmakas
Ακρ. Αγ. Γιάννης
Ag. Giannis Cape
Ακρ. Μέλισσα
Melissa Cape
ΟΡΜΟΣ ΑΦΑΛΕΣ
AFALES BAY
ΟΡΜΟΣ ΦΡΙΚΕΣ
FRIKES BAY
Ακρ. Αργαστάρyες
Argastarges Cape
Αγ. Σαράντα
Ag. Saranda
Μεσοβούνι
Messovouni
Λαχός
Lachos
Ακρωτήρι
Akrotiri Cape
ΟΡΜΟΣ ΚΙΟΝΙ
KIONI BAY
Κάλαμος
Kalamos
Κόλλιέρη
Kollieri
Εξοχή
Exoyi
Πλατρειθιάς
Platrithias
Φρικές
Frikees
Ράχη
Rachi
Κιόνι
Kioni
Ακ. Αγ. Ηλίας
Ag. Ilias Cape
Μ. Μερνοράκια
Pernarakia Mon.
Περναράκια
Pernarakia
Καλύβια
Kalyvia
Πηλικάτα
Pilikata
ΣΠΗΛΑΙΟ ΛΟΥΙΖΟΥ
LOUIZOS CAVE
Σταυρός
Stavros
Ανωγή
Anoyi
Ακρ. Ιερουσαλήμ
Ierousalim Cape
ΠΟΡΤΟ ΝΙΚΟΥΤΣΟ
PORTO NIKOUTSO
Νηριτός
Niritos
Λευκή
Lefki
Μονή Καθαρά
Kathara Mon.
ITHAKI'S CHANNEL
ΣΤΕΝΑ ΙΘΑΚΗΣ
Ακρ. Βαρδιόλα
Vardiola Cape
Ακρ. Πιδάκι
Gidaki Cape
SKINOS BAY
Ακρ. Αγ. Ανδρέας
Ag. Andreas Cape
Βαθύ
Vathi
AETOS BAY
Αγ. Ιωάννης
Ag. Ioannis
ΑΓΡΟΣ ΛΑΕΡΤΗ
LAERTIS' FIELD
Ακρ. Αγ. Γιάννης
Ag. Giannis Cape
Δεξιά
Dexia
Αετός
Aetos
ΣΠΗΛΑΙΟ ΝΥΜΦΩΝ
NYMFON CAVE
Παλαιοχώρα
Paleochora
ΑΛΑΛΚΟΜΕΝΕΣ
ALALKOMENES
Περαχώρι
Perachori
ΑΡΕΘΟΥΣΑ ΠΗΓΗ
ARETHOUSSA SOURCE
ΒΡΑΧΟΣ ΚΟΡΑΚΑ
KORAKAS ROCK
ΚΑΛΥΒΙ
EVMEOS
ΟΡΜΟΣ ΠΙΣΩ ΑΕΤΟΥ
PISO AETOS BAY
Μονή Ταξιαρχών
Taxiarchon Mon.
ΟΡΜΟΣ ΑΝΔΡΙ
ANDRI BAY
Ακρ. Δαφνούδι
Dafnoudi Bay
Φισκάρδο
Fiskardo
Γερμενάτα
Germenata
Αντίπατα
Antipata
Καστανάτα
Kastarata
Τσελεντάτα
Tselentata
Μάγγανος
Manganos
Βεντουράτα
Ventourata
Ευρέτη
Erreti
Χαλικέρι
Chalikeri
Τζαμαρελάτα
Tzamarelata
Βιγλί
Vigli
Κονιδαράτα
Konidarata
Μαρκουλάτα
Markoulata
Τουλιάτα
Touliata
Βασιλικιάδες
Vassilikiades
Μεσοβούνια
Messovounia
Δραπανίτικα
Drapanitika
Πλαγιά
Playia
Κόθριας
Kothrias
Κοκολάτα
Kokolata
Βαρύ
Vary
Δεφαρανάτα
Defaranata
Καριά
Karia
Άσσος
Assos
Κομιτάτα
Komitata
Πατρικάτα
Patrikata
Μονή Θεματων
Thematon Mon.
Καλόν Ορος
Kalon Oros
Νεοχώρι
Neochori
Ανωμεριά
Anomeria
Καρουσάτα
Karoussata
Φερεδινάτα
Feredinata
Ξηροπόταμος
Kseropotamos
Δρακάτα
Drakata
Αντίπατα
Antipata
Δενδρινάτα
Dendrinata
Αγ. Ευφημία
St. Efimia
ΟΡΜΟΣ ΑΓ. ΕΥΦΗΜΙΑ
AG. EFIMIA BAY
Ποταμιανάτα
Potamianata
Μακριώτικα
Makriotika
Δρακοπουλάτα
Drakopoulata
Ακρ. Κακάτα
Kakata Cape
Ακρ. Αθέρας
Atheras Cape
ΟΡΜΟΣ ΜΥΡΤΟΣ
MYRTOS BAY
MYRTOS BEACH
ΟΡΜΟΣ ΣΑΜΗΣ
SAMI BAY
Ακρ. Διχαλιά
Dichalia Cape
Ακρ. Αγριλιά
Agrilia Cape
Antisamos
Αντίσαμος
Μονή Αγριλίων
Agrilion Mon.
Αγ. Σπυρίδων
Ag. Spyridon
Αθέρας
Atheras
Αγ. Κυριακή
Ag. Kyriaki
Ζολά
Zola
Αγκώνας
Angonas
Μονή Θεοτόκου
Theotokos Mon.
Καραβόμυλος
Karavomylosi
ΣΠΗΛΑΙΟ ΜΕΛΙΣΑΝΗ
MELISSANI CAVE
Σάμη
Sami
Νύφη
Nifi
Πετρικάτα
Petrikata
Καρδακάτα
Kardakata
Ρίζα
Riza
Αγ. Δυνατή
Ag. Dynati
ΣΠΗΛΑΙΟ ΔΡΟΓΚΑΡΑΤΙ
DROGARATI CAVE
Πουλάτα
Poulata
Ζερβάτα
Vlachata
Κόκκινη Ράχ
Kokkini Rach
Κοντογουράτα
Kontogourata
Γκριζάτα
Grizata
Χαλιωτάτα
Chaliotata
Κουλουράτα
Koulourata
Ευμορφία
Evmorfia
Κουρουκλάτα
Kourouklata
PETANI BAY
ΟΡΜΟΣ ΠΕΤΑΝΗ
PETANI BEACH
Ακρ. Ορθολίθια
Ortholithia Cape
Δειλινάτα
Dilinata
Τσακαρισιάνος
Tsakarisianos
Λιβάδι
Livadi
Κοντογενάδα
Kontogenada
Κουβαλάτα
Kouvalata
Φάρσα
Farsa
Βιλατόρια
Vilatoria
Αγ. Δημήτριος
Ag. Dimitrios
Δαυγάτα
Davgata
Φαρακλάτα
Faraklata
Αγ. Θέκλα
Ag. Thekla
Σκινιάς
Skinias
Φραγάτα
Fragata
Αγ. Ελευθέριος
Ag. Eleftherios
Καλάτα
Kalata
Δελαπορτάτα
Delaportata
Ληξούρι
Lixouri
Μονή Κεχριόνος
Kechrionos Mon.
ΚΑΤΑΒΟΘΡΕΣ
KATAVOTHES
Προκοπάτα
Prokopata
Ραζάτα
Razata
Βαλσαμάτα
Valsamata
Μιχάτα
Michata
Επανωχώρι
Epanochori
Καμιναράτα
Kaminarata
Φαβατάτα
Favatata
Αργοστόλι
Argostoli
Μονή Αγ. Γερασίμου
Gerasimou Mon.
Τρωιανάτα
Troianata
Χαβδάτα
Chavdata
Σουλάρι
Soulari
Μιχαλιτσάτα
Michalitsata
Δεμουτσαδάτα
Dermoutsadata
Μιτακάτα
Mitakata
Μουσάτα
Moussata
ΒΛΑΧΑΤΑ
VLAXATA
Σιμωτάτ
Simotat
SUNSET VIEW
ΗΛΙΟΒΑΣΙΛΕΜΑ
Μονή Ταφίων
Tafion Mon.
Λάσι
Lasi
Τραυλιάτα
Travliata
Κάστρο
Kastro
Καραβάδος
Karavados
Λουρδάτα
Lourdata
Μονή Κηπουραίων
Kipoureon Mon.
Βουνί
Vouni
Μαντζαβινάτα
Mantzavinata
Λεπέδα
Lepeda
Κοβοθεκράτα
Kovothekrata
Περατάτα
Peratata
Χαβριάτα
Chavriata
Μονή Αγ. Παρασκευής
St. Paraskevi Mon.
Μονή Εσταυρωμένου
Estavromenou Mon.
Ακρ. Γερογόμπος
Gerogobos Cape
Ακρ. Αγ. Γεώργιος
Ag. Georgios Cape
Λακήθρα
Lakithra
Μεταξάτα
Metaxata
Κεραμιές
Keramies
Πεσσάδα
Pessada
ΟΡΜΟΣ ΛΟΥΡΔΑΣ
LOURDA BAY
Ξι
Ksi
Μηνιές
Minies
Σπαρτιά
Spartia
Σβορωνάτα
Svoronata
Κουρκουμελάτα
Kourkoumelata
Ν. ΒΑΡΔΙΑΝΗ
VARDIANI ISL.
ΣΑΡΛΑΤΑ
SARLATA
Κοριανά
Koriana
Ακρωτήρι
Akrotiri Cape
Ν. ΔΙΑΣ
DIAS ISL.
ΠΡΟΣ ΖΑΚ
TO ZAKY

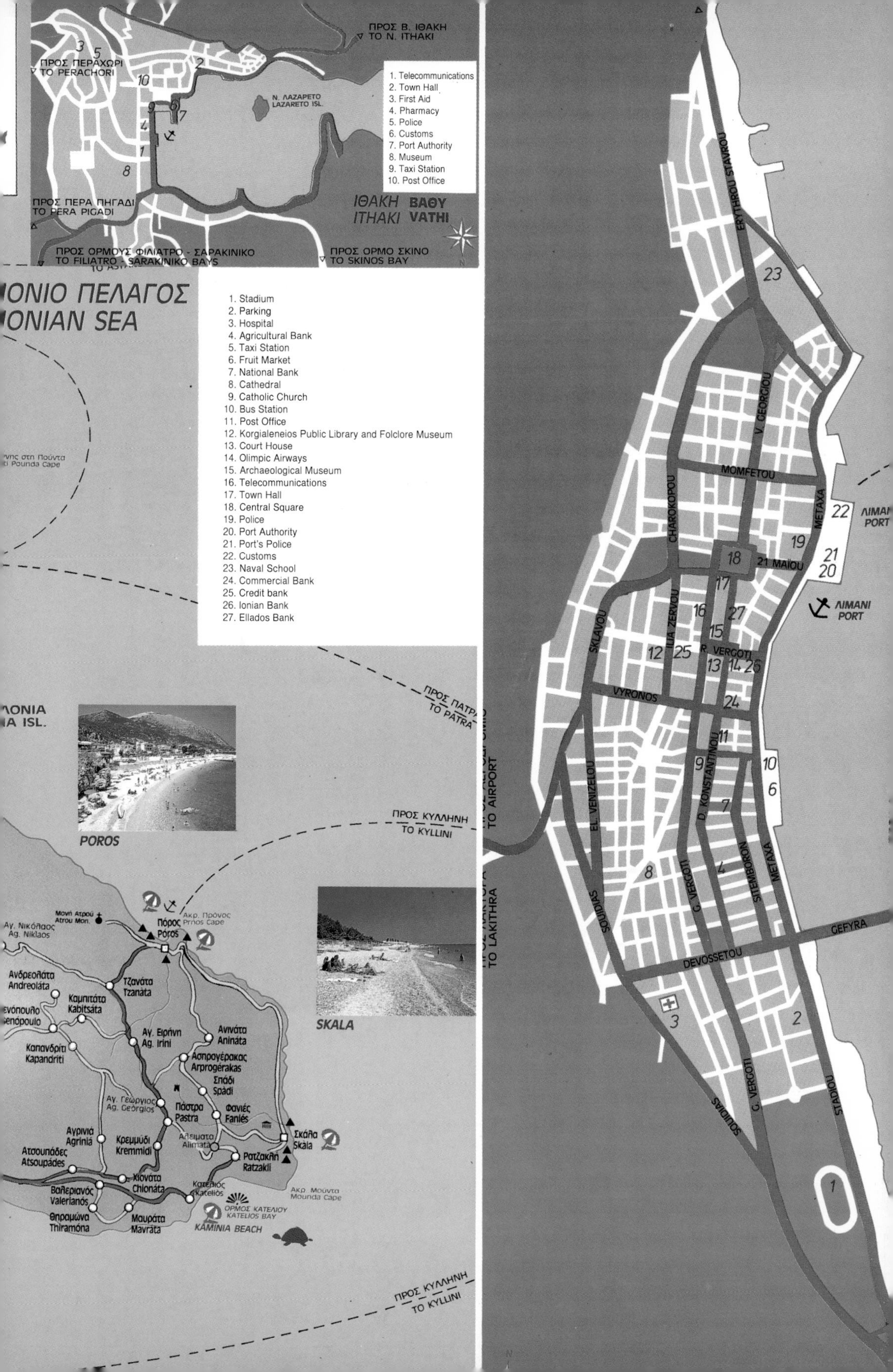

ΠΡΟΣ Β. ΙΘΑΚΗ
TO N. ITHAKI
ΠΡΟΣ ΠΕΡΑΧΩΡΙ
TO PERACHORI
Ν. ΛΑΖΑΡΕΤΟ
LAZARETO ISL.
1. Telecommunications
2. Town Hall
3. First Aid
4. Pharmacy
5. Police
6. Customs
7. Port Authority
8. Museum
9. Taxi Station
10. Post Office
ΠΡΟΣ ΠΕΡΑ ΠΗΓΑΔΙ
TO PERA PIGADI
ΙΘΑΚΗ ΒΑΘΥ
ITHAKI VATHI
ΠΡΟΣ ΟΡΜΟΥΣ ΦΙΛΙΑΤΡΟ - ΣΑΡΑΚΙΝΙΚΟ
TO FILIATRO - SARAKINIKO BAYS
ΠΡΟΣ ΟΡΜΟ ΣΚΙΝΟ
TO SKINOS BAY
ΙΟΝΙΟ ΠΕΛΑΓΟΣ
IONIAN SEA
1. Stadium
2. Parking
3. Hospital
4. Agricultural Bank
5. Taxi Station
6. Fruit Market
7. National Bank
8. Cathedral
9. Catholic Church
10. Bus Station
11. Post Office
12. Korgialeneios Public Library and Folclore Museum
13. Court House
14. Olimpic Airways
15. Archaeological Museum
16. Telecommunications
17. Town Hall
18. Central Square
19. Police
20. Port Authority
21. Port's Police
22. Customs
23. Naval School
24. Commercial Bank
25. Credit bank
26. Ionian Bank
27. Ellados Bank
ΠΡΟΣ ΠΑΤΡΑ
TO PATRA
ΠΡΟΣ ΚΥΛΛΗΝΗ
TO KYLLINI
TO AIRPORT
TO LAKITHRA
POROS
SKALA
Μονή Ατρού
Atrou Mon.
Πόρος
Poros
Ακρ. Πρόνος
Prnos Cape
Αγ. Νικόλαος
Ag. Niklaos
Ανδρεολάτα
Andreoláta
Τζανάτα
Tzanáta
Καμπιτάτα
Kabitsáta
Αγ. Ειρήνη
Ag. Irini
Ανινάτα
Aninàta
Καπανδρίτι
Kapandriti
Ασπρογέρακας
Arprogérakas
Σπάθί
Spádi
Αγ. Γεώργιος
Ag. Georgios
Πάστρα
Pastra
Φανιές
Faniés
Αγρινιά
Agriniá
Κρεμμύδι
Kremmidi
Αλείματα
Alimatá
Σκάλα
Skala
Ατσουπάδες
Atsoupádes
Ρατζακλί
Ratzakli
Χιονάτα
Chionáta
Βαλεριανός
Valerianós
Κατελειός
Katelios
Ακρ. Μούντα
Mounda Cape
ΟΡΜΟΣ ΚΑΤΕΛΙΟΥ
KATELIOS BAY
Θηραμώνα
Thiramóna
Μαυράτα
Mavráta
KAMINIA BEACH
ERYTHROU STAVROU
V. GEORGIOU
MOMFETOU
CHAROKOPOU
METAXA
ΛΙΜΑΝΙ
PORT
21 MAIOU
ILIA ZERVOU
SKLAVOU
R. VERGOTI
VYRONOS
D. KONSTANTINOU
EL. VENIZELOU
G. VERGOTI
SITEMBORON
SOUIDIAS
DEVOSSETOU
GEFYRA
STADIOU